50
Weekend
Garden
Projects

D0198491

50 Weekend Garden Projects

TOBY BUCKLAND

PHOTOGRAPHY BY
HOWARD RICE

CASSELL
ILLUSTRATED

First published in paperback in 2003 by Cassell Illustrated

Text copyright © 2001 Toby Buckland
Design and layout copyright © 2001 Cassell & Co

The moral right of Toby Buckland to be identified as the author of this
work has been asserted in accordance with the Copyright, Designs and
Patents Act of 1988

All rights reserved. No part of this publication may be reproduced in any
material form (including photocopying or storing it in any medium by
electronic means and whether or not transiently or incidentally to some
other use of this publication) without the written permission of the
copyright owner, except in accordance with the provisions of the
Copyright, Designs and Patents Act 1988 or under the terms of a licence
issued by the Copyright Licensing Agency, 90 Tottenham Court Road,
London W1P 9HE. Applications for the copyright owner's written
permission to reproduce any part of this publication should be addressed
to the publisher.

All photography by Howard Rice
Designed by Grade Design Consultants

A CIP catalogue record for this book is available from the
British Library

ISBN 1 84403 062 8

Printed and bound in Hong Kong

Cassell Illustrated
A Member of Octopus Publishing Group Ltd
2-4 Heron Quays
London
E14 4JP

Contents

Introduction

For me, the thrill of gardening lies in realising the potential of plants, places and materials, which at first glance seem unpromising, and turning them into something special, something new.

Creating new gardens or features within them is always enjoyable, not just because of the pleasure they give once they are made but also due to the excitement and fun of making them.

What holds many people back from really enjoying gardening is lack of know-how and time. That's why *50 Weekend Garden Projects* contains projects ranging in size from a whole weekend down to just a few minutes, listing all the tools, plants and materials you'll need and breaking each down into simple steps.

Some projects are designed to beautify a garden and some to make it more practical and productive. There are features for all styles including cottage, children's and modern gardens as well as ideas to celebrate each of the seasons.

I hope this book will inspire gardeners to try their hand at fresh ideas and explore new materials but, most of all, realise the potential of their own gardens.

Toby Buckland

Spring always starts slowly and the

becomes a rush towards summer. The once bare earth is now knee-deep in fresh green foliage and spring flowers, all within the space of a few weeks.

More plants come into flower at this time than any other and woodland walks are spectacular as Bluebells, Wood Anemones and Primroses effortlessly stage a flower show before the trees leaf up. Not all plants are so self-sufficient though, and many climbers and tall herbaceous plants need a little help and guidance now to look their best later on.

Alpine plants come into bloom at this time and many of these miniature marvels lend themselves to creating colourful plant pictures and sculptures, being sufficiently tough even for young children to model.

Spring is a time for thinking ahead too. Sow seeds for flowers and platefuls of fresh vegetables later and prepare the patio for the first alfresco meals and parties of the year.

Spring

Stained Glass Trellis

For the best array of coloured shadows, capture the sun at its lowest – either in the morning or late afternoon – by positioning the trellis on a south-east or south-west boundary.

Stained glass has its origins in antiquity: for millennia, it has been used to decorate the windows of palaces and temples. As light passes through it, the glass shines like gem stones and projects coloured shadows onto neighbouring walls and floors. Some of the pigments that colour the glass are precious: for example, silver is used to stain the glass red. But whatever colours you use, it will create a look of luxury. Stained glass combined with a trellis will transform existing boundaries or customise new ones. It's easy to fit and can be bought cut-to-size from most glaziers. The trellis shown here could be used as a screen or a coping to an existing fence to give extra privacy. If you want to limit the cost, only put the glass in strategic sections of trellis – for example in arches or in squares surrounding a focal point like a statue or water feature.

You will need...

Trellis panels
Blue wood stain
Stained glass rectangles
12mm wood screws
2cm strips of 3mm marine ply
Drill
Screwdriver

1. Order glass from a glazier, having first measured the average of the trellis squares and then adding on two centimetres to one side. This gives you a rectangle shape, rather than a square, which will sit between the spars of the trellis but won't fall through the holes.

2. Paint both sides of the trellis with wood stain and allow to dry. Wood stain is available in lots of colours, so choose one that will complement the colours of your stained glass.

3. Put the trellis face down on the ground or lean it against a wall and arrange the glass into patterns, sitting it between the horizontals and leaning it up against the uprights.

4. Cut the marine ply into strips that are 1–2mm thinner than the wood in the trellis. This is to create battens which will hold the glass in place but won't be visible from the front. Pilot two holes – one in the top and one in the bottom – through them and into the outside edge of the uprights keeping away from the glass. Then fix in position with the screws.

Furniture Paint Effects

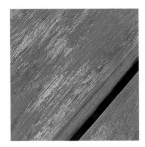

Try rubbing a pebble as well as sandpaper over the table to blend the paint and create a richer tapestry of colours.

With the trend towards outdoor living, the choice and range of outdoor furniture has vastly increased. But if you want to keep down the price of having individual-looking chairs and tables or if you want to bring an old table that's past its best back to life, distressed paint effects are the answer. The distressed look gives furniture a naturally weathered appearance but also makes it rich in colour and interesting to look at. Choose the base colour according to the style of garden you have – blue for Mediterranean, red for Japanese, green for classic or natural designs. Painting is a good way of adding harmony to a garden as it will unite furniture collected from different ranges or link it with garden features such as sheds, arbours or glazed pots. It will also extend its life, make it more inviting and tailor it uniquely to your tastes.

You will need...

Tin of acrylic scumble glaze
0.5L of white emulsion paint
1L of blue paint
0.5L of acrylic varnish
Sandpaper and paint brushes

Preparation...

If you're painting furniture that has been treated with a coloured wood stain or gloss, sand away as much of it as possible to create a good key for the emulsion. Wood stains and gloss paints aren't suitable for scumbling, so stick to emulsions and protect from the weather with a layer of varnish.

1. Sandpaper the picnic table to remove grease and to give the paint a key.

2. Paint the table with blue emulsion paint (green also works well) and allow to dry. You don't have to be too particular how this is done so it won't matter if some bits are streaky.

3. Mix a 50/50 solution of white emulsion paint and scumble glaze. The scumble makes the paint dry slowly, giving you more time to work it.

4. Paint the table with a thin coat of scumble-emulsion mix. Again, the more uneven the coat, the better. Let it dry for a couple of minutes.

5. Gently wipe over the table with a damp cloth until a patchwork of blue shows through while leaving traces of white in the grain.

6. Then go over the table with sandpaper to accentuate the different patches of colour. The aim is to create as many shades of colour between blue to white as you can plus the odd patch where the wood grain shows through.

7. Once you've achieved the paint effect you like, apply an acrylic varnish to protect the table from the elements.

Screens

No matter how tidy or colourful your garden, an ugly chain-link fence such as this will ruin the effect.

An attractive boundary fence can make all the difference to how your garden looks and feels, giving windswept sites shelter, overlooked gardens privacy and untidy plots unity, as well as clearly dividing your garden from the neighbours'.

In the back garden a post and panel fence will achieve all these things, but in the front garden they can look out of place. Until recently the only alternative was a palisade or a chain-link fence, which looks terrible in a garden setting. But now, willow screen is available from garden centres and makes for a fabulous fence that looks good, allows light through it and is easy to put up.

You will need*...

Rolls of 1m x 3m willow screen**
Plastic-coated 3mm wire, 3 times
 the length of the fencing run
Roll of 1mm garden wire
6 bolt tensioners
Pliers
Hacksaw and file if the tops are uneven
Thin plank of wood

*   For 1m of fence.
**   Willow screen is also available in 1.5m x 3m rolls
        and can be cut down the middle to make a shorter
        but more economical fence.

Attaching the screen to wooden posts...

The easiest way to install the screen is to attach it to existing fence posts. In my front garden these were metal, but the screen would look just as good running between wooden posts.

To do this, attach the wire to vine eyes screwed into the end posts, and run it through holes drilled through the middle posts. Tighten the wire using an 'in-line' wire tensioner, available from hardware shops, and cut the willow screen to fit between the posts, fixing in position with thin garden wire.

1. Remove the old fencing leaving the posts intact. Replace any that are loose or rotten and, if their heights fluctuate, cut them level with a hacksaw and file off any sharp edges.

2. Paint metal posts with a rust-proofing paint. The quickest way is to use an aerosol, reducing 'drift' with a piece of old newspaper.

3. Drill three lines of holes through each post – one in the middle, one 10cm down from the top and one 10cm up from the bottom – using a metal drill bit. Run three lines of the 3mm wire through the holes and attach the ends to bolt tensioners fixed through the end posts.

4. Prop the fence against the wires sitting its base on a plank of wood to keep it proud of the soil while it is tied in position with thin garden wire. Aim to put a tie in every 20cm on the top wire and every 30cm on the lower two.

Plant Planets

A plant planet never fails to impress visitors no matter what the season.
Made from two hanging baskets planted with house leeks and wired together, it always looks colourful and architectural. Best of all, unlike normal hanging baskets, it never needs watering. In fact, the only maintenance is filling the gaps left as the odd rosette fades after flowering.

Hang in a sunny position outside a door or from a pergola. Better still, suspend from a tree as though in orbit above a border, where it will sway as the wind blows.

You will need...

2 small hanging baskets
Roll of thin garden wire
35 1L pots of house leeks, choose
 pots with 5–10 2cm rosettes per pot
Pliers
Bag of moss
Multipurpose compost
30cm x 30cm square of cardboard or
 fibre board
2 plastic pots, roughly 20cm across the rim

Flowers for globes...

Alternatives to house leeks include summer bedding plants such as Busy Lizzies, bedding verbenas, mesembryanthemum and petunias. To make watering easier, nestle a small pot among the roots of the plants with its rim pressed against the wire of the basket, below the point at which the chain is attached. This then acts as a funnel, allowing water to be poured into the heart of the basket without running off its surface. Pinch out wayward-growing tips through the summer to keep the stems dense and encourage flowering.

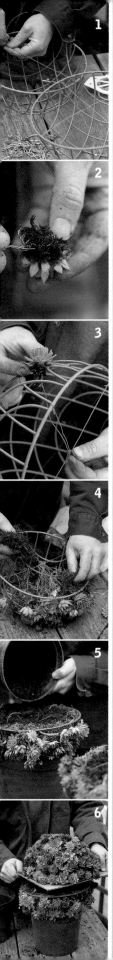

1. Remove the chains from the hanging baskets and tie two cross-wires to their rims making sure that the wire is tight and held firmly in place.

2. Divide the pots of house leeks into individual rosettes, keeping as much root on them as possible. Cut 15cm lengths of wire and loop around the rosettes, just below the leaves holding them firmly but without damaging them.

3. Hook each rosette into the wire frame of the hanging basket with the leaves facing out and the roots pointing inwards. Tie in place by bending the wire attached to the house leek around the wire across the centre of the basket. Repeat the process until you have a group of roughly 20 house leeks. Don't worry if the wire at the centre of the basket is becoming like a bird's nest, as this is normal!

4. Pack a 2cm layer of moss in among the roots to cover the wires so that they cannot be seen from the outside and to hold the house leeks in place. Then continue tying in, packing with moss as you go.

5. When both baskets are complete, sit them in plastic pots so that they are flat and fill with multi-purpose compost.

6. Place the fibre board over one of the baskets so that the compost is held as you flip it over on top of the other basket. Pull out the board carefully and tie the two rims of the basket together with wire and re-attach the chain to the rim. Then hang the globe in a sunny place.

Patio Makeover

An economical and stylish solution for covering ugly concrete patios can be made from timber planks and gravel. This technique is particularly useful for terraced and semi-detached houses, which often have alleys that are difficult to deal with along the back of the house. But it can be used to cover any concrete patio, provided the edge of the gravel is shuttered in to stop it getting kicked about.

You can modify the size of the squares and paint the timber to suit your taste. Dark timber combined with pale gravel creates an oriental/Tudor look. Or why not create an abstract modern Mondrianesque effect with a patchwork of primary-coloured squares?

You will need...

Weed-suppressing mat (as big
 as the area you want to makeover)
Treated timber planks
Drill and masonry bit
Rawlplugs and 50mm screws
Screwdriver
Hammer
Wood saw
Two shades of gravel
Large pebbles for dressing, optional

1. Clear pots, chairs and tables from the area and sweep over to remove soil and stones. Spread weed-suppressing membrane over the area, leaving any drains uncovered for access.

2. Cut the timber planks into sets of four equal lengths and arrange into squares over the membrane avoiding drains.

3. Drill two holes through the ends of each plank and 40mm into the concrete below.

4. Push a Rawlplug into each hole and turn a screw into their tops. Hammer through the timber until just the last centimetre is left proud.

5. Screw the last centimetre home with a screwdriver making sure that the top of the screw is recessed below the surface of the wood.

6. Gravel the insides of the squares using one colour of gravel, and the outsides with another to accentuate the patchwork effect.

Hazel and Willow Spirals

Using hazel and willow to create supports for sweet peas and runner beans is a long-standing cottage garden tradition. Even in today's gardens, they have their place, making a garden look mature, giving flat borders a focal point and supporting climbing plants that would otherwise clamber on a wall or trellis. Hazel will outlast the modern alternative of bamboo by many years and will fit into any part of the garden. Hazel poles on their own can look sparse in winter: to make them more decorative, spiral willow up between them.

You will need...

5 2m hazel rods (available from
 some garden centres, thatching companies
 and woodland trusts)
Small bundle of willow
Secateurs

About hazel and willow...

Hundreds of thousands of hazel rods used to be cut from woodlands every year as they were, and still are, used to make spars for thatched roofs and to centre cob walls. Only thin rods are of any use, so trees would be cut down to ground level and the subsequent hedgehog of regrowth harvested every five years or so. Contrary to what you might think, the plants thrive on this regime, living longer than if they had never been cut. The technique, called coppicing, is still carried out by thatchers and woodland trusts who often have the hazel for sale. Willow can be bought mail order or you can use prunings from garden plants like dogwood or jasmine.

1. Mark a circle on the ground about 45cm wide and push the thick end of the hazel rods into the soil, evenly spaced around the circle.

2. Bring the tops together and tie with string. Then cut the rods to the same height and bind over the string with a length of willow, jamming the end between the rods to hold it firm.

3. Starting at the bottom of the wigwam take two lengths of willow and hold one each side of a hazel rod. Then plait them together, winding them around each other three or four times and pass them either side of the next rod.

4. When you have gone as far as you can go with the first two lengths of willow, wrap new lengths around the part of the spiral that has been done, jamming their ends between the plaits to secure them. Continue this process up the wigwam, adjusting the pitch of the spiral as you go.

5. Once you have reached the top and the helix looks right to you, wind more willow over the plaited sections, bind any loose parts together and then cut off any untidy ends with secateurs.

Woodland Path

Tip... Apart from a watering in the first season to get new plants established, raking out leaves in autumn, and giving an annual mulch of compost, woodland gardens need very little looking after.

Planting beneath the shade of trees and shrubs can daunt even a seasoned gardener, but with the right structure and the right plants in place, woodland gardening is very easy and satisfying. Log-edged bark paths make simple and effective frameworks, dividing borders and creating a natural woodland feel. They are also practical, enabling extra compost to be piled into the beds, replicating the cover of woodland leaf litter.

There are hundreds of interesting plants to choose for a shady patch, all available from garden centres but originally harking from woodland habitats. These are plants that have developed tactics to help them survive in the shade. Bulbs such as wood anemones, bluebells and winter aconites flower early in the year, taking advantage of the high light levels when deciduous trees are bare. Epimediums, bergenias and tellima have tough evergreen leaves rich in light-catching chlorophyll and they too flower before the trees leaf up. However, not all shade dwellers flower in winter and spring: foxgloves and sweet rocket bloom in June, and monkshood, tiger lilies and Japanese anemones flower right into autumn. Choose plants carefully and a woodland garden will look good throughout the year.

You will need...

Branches 10–20cm thick*
Bark chips, approximately 1 80L bag
 for every 4 square metres of path
Hosepipe

Spade
Wood saw
Rake

* Buy them from tree surgeons.

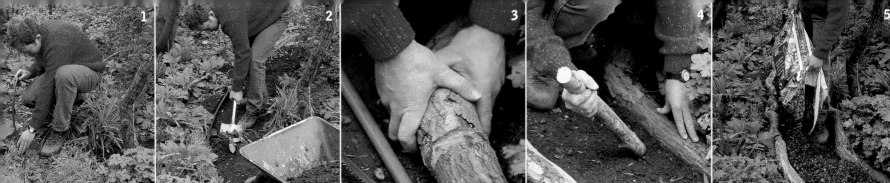

1. Mark out the path edges with the hosepipe. Then stand back and make sure that it looks good when viewed from the house and elsewhere in the garden. Paths lead the eye so make sure yours doesn't lead to an unattractive building or eyesore in the far distance. Make the path at least 70cm wide so that walking along it is comfortable.

2. Dig out the base of the path by about 6cm and pile the soil into the borders. Getting the borders deep in soil and compost is essential to create the right growing conditions for woodland plants.

3. Lay the logs along the edge of the path, butting together those with similar diameters.

4. Ram soil along the sides of the logs with a branch or hammer handle. This keeps them held firmly in place.

5. Put bark down between the logs and the path is complete.

Patio Vegetable Garden

Other plants to try...
Basil (above, top) and loose-leaf lettuce (above, bottom) both work well, but also worth considering are beetroot, radish, spinach, dwarf beans, mangetout, windowsill carrots, sweet and chilli peppers, Chinese cabbage, mustard, pak choi, mizuna greens, parsley, thyme and coriander.

Harvesting fresh vegetables straight from the garden is one of the highlights of summer, and you don't need a huge vegetable patch to do it. Many vegetable varieties grow quite happily in pots, sometimes producing better crops than plants in the ground. A pot of veg on a patio, for example, is less susceptible to slugs, but if they do attack the slugs are easier to find and kill. And although there is less space and smaller harvests, a pot can be situated right outside the kitchen door, making picking to cook incredibly convenient. Vegetables can be attractive plants: lettuce leaves can vary in shade from green to purple; and trusses of cherry tomatoes are shapely and bright. Marigolds will add colour and attract pest predators, such as hoverflies, which are drawn to the flowers and then hunt over the vegetables picking off aphids.

Pick the beans and tomatoes regularly to encourage more to form, and harvest the lettuce by pulling it from the compost, making space for other plants to grow. Keep well watered throughout the summer.

You will need...

Large pot or half-barrel
3 1.5m straight pencil-thin twigs
Raffia or string
John Innes No3 and multi-purpose compost
Climbing French beans, 'Tumbler' tomatoes,
 loose-leaf lettuce, basil, marigolds,
 strawberries or ruby chard

1. Place the pot in a sunny position and cover the drainage holes with a layer of stones. Fill with John Innes and multi-purpose compost, mixing them together as you go. The John Innes gives the mix body – holding extra water and nutrients – and the multi-purpose givews it bulk.

2. Push the twigs right into the compost in a triangle arrangement and tie the tops together with raffia or string.

3. Plant a climbing French bean at the base of each twig, leaning the top towards the twig to encourage it to climb.

4. Edge around the beans with the chard, lettuce, strawberries, basil and tomatoes.

5. Plant marigolds for colour in the middle and water the plants to wash the compost in among their roots. After three to four weeks, feed once a fortnight with a diluted liquid fertilizer.

Cherry Tomato Fans

Getting the most from tomatoes... To encourage tomatoes to ripen, pinch out the growing tip when the plants reach the top of the bamboo canes and pick as soon as they are ripe to ensure a succession of crops right through the summer. Water and feed regularly with liquid tomato fertiliser.

If I could grow only one type of vegetable it would be cherry tomato. They crop with abundance and taste sweeter in sauces and salads than any other tomato. They're also expensive to buy from the supermarket and, by growing my own, I can have a selection of varieties, each with its own flavour. A few years ago I was stuck for growing space and wanted an easy way to grow a range of different tomatoes. So I made a wooden planter (see page 66) and grew them as cordons – trained up a cane – in a fan arrangement. It worked so well, that I've done it every year since. A large wooden planter makes an ideal home for tomatoes: it looks good on the patio and contains a large reservoir of compost that doesn't dry out quickly. It also offers space for marigolds or lettuce to grow at their feet. Either grow your own tomatoes from seed sown in April, or buy ready-grown plants from garden centres. Only plant outside when the risk of frost has gone – usually late May or early June depending where you live – and when the first flowers have been pollinated and tiny tomatoes are visible. Planting or feeding before this time encourages lots of leafy growth at the expense of flowers and fruit.

You will need...

5 tomato plants, preferably different varieties
5 marigold plants
5 garden canes
2 bags of compost

Soft gardener's twine
Garden trowel
Large wooden planter*

* To make and decorate a wooden planter see page 66

1. Fill the planter with compost and make a fan of bamboo canes by pushing them into the compost at the back of the planter. Then plant marigolds along the front and a tomato at the base of each cane.

2. Select a 'leader', or main stem, for each tomato plant and, as they grow, tie them to the bamboo cane using soft garden twine.

3. Dead-head the marigolds regularly and remove any side shoots growing off the main stem of the tomato plants by pinching them out between your fingers. Look for them above the junction where the leaves meet the stem.

Herbaceous Plant Hoops

The season starts for herbaceous plants such as delphiniums, asters and phlox in early spring when their shoots emerge, breaking the cold brown earth with their fresh green leaves. As the days draw out, growth becomes incredibly fast: each day their expansion is noticeable, until most of the soil is covered. Then, as summer arrives, the shoots send up flower spikes and the summer flower show begins.

Tall-growing delphiniums and asters need to be staked to stop their stems toppling over in summer storms, while herbaceous plants with heavy blooms, such as peonies, dahlias and lupins, need extra bracing to prevent them buckling under the weight of their own flowers. Do this when the plants are about 30cm tall, so that they can grow into, and hide, their support. Conspicuous wire staking systems are available from garden centres, but supports fashioned from willow, or the prunings from late-winter-flowering shrubs blend more naturally with the plants that grow through them.

You will need...

10 1m pencil-thin stems of willow, dogwood,
 winter-flowering jasmine, forsythia or flowering currant
String
Secateurs
3 bamboo canes per hoop

1. Plait two stems together to make a hoop roughly 60cm across. If the stems keep unravelling, tie the two ends together with string before you start.

2. Tightly wind more stems around the hoop building up the thickness of its sides.

3. Poke straight pieces of stem – if you don't have any, use thin bamboo – through the plaited sides of the hoop to make a '#' shape in the middle. If these rods seem loose, bind around the plaited stems with string until they are firm

4. Cut any excess off the '#' with secateurs and poke three bamboo canes up through the sides of the hoop to make the legs.

5. Push the canes into the soil above a herbaceous plant. As the plant grows, slide the hoop up until it is 5cm from the top of the canes. Store in a shed over winter and use again the following year.

The Green Man

Care... The Green Man is trouble-free to keep. Water directly after planting and position him in the garden where he'll get plenty of sun. From time to time, the straggly plants may need to be cut back, particularly if they start to cover his face. After all, we all need occasional grooming to look our best.

The Green Man was a mythical figure who represented the forces of Nature in pre-Christian Europe. He is a common figure in Celtic art, a symbol of fertility and the changing seasons. His beard and hair are usually portrayed as a wild mane of leaves, so his image lends itself to creating a picture from living plants.

The mystery of the Green Man is something that appeals to the imagination of young and old alike, so you might want to involve the kids. The rockery plants chosen for this project are all tough succulents, which cope with young, unskilled hands teasing them apart.

The plants used here came from a garden centre, but if you have a rockery you may already have some fleshy-leaved succulent plants that you can take divisions of and use.

You will need...

4 pots of green house leeks
2 pots of red house leeks
Pot of Sedum acre minor
2 pots of Sedum 'Coral Carpet'
3 pots of Mesembryanthemum 'Basutoland'
Pebble
Small bag of horticultural grit
60cm terracotta 'pan' or wide pot.

1. Cover the hole in the bottom of the pan with stones and fill it with compost, adding two or three handfuls of horticultural grit to improve the drainage. Then cover the surface of the compost with a thin layer of grit.

2. Sprinkle compost onto the grit to mark out the features of the Green Man's face, making sure there is plenty of room to plant 'hair' above his eyes.

3. Divide the house leeks up into individual crowns and the mat-forming plants like the Sedum into small clumps, gently easing the roots apart in your hands. Don't worry if you lose most of the roots and compost as the plants will soon recover.

4. Plant up the face, pushing individual crowns and small clumps through the grit into the compost. Use green house leeks for the cheeks and forehead and red for the lips and ears.

5. Build up the beard and hair around the face with the Sedum and use the more straggly mesembryanthemum towards the edge of the pot. A long pebble nose and white and black stone eyes bring the Green Man to life.

House Leek Planters

Finished look... House leek planters look wonderful in containers, forming coral-like reefs packed with rosettes or making impenetrable carpets over the surface of compost.

House leeks or Sempervivums can be found for sale in the Alpine section of garden centres between the Sedums and the silene. Although cactus-like in appearance, they don't come from the desert but from Turkistan, where they grow, among other places, between cracks in roof tiles. There are hundreds of varieties to choose from, in colours ranging through green, copper, red and purple. Some change colour with the season; others have silk-like webbing between their leaves. When a rosette reaches maturity it flowers, producing a spike topped with daisy-like blooms, and then it dies. But the gap is soon filled by offsets that form around the rosette during its life.

You will need...

30cm square pot
20cm round pot (this is optional but
 accentuates the colour difference
 between the house leeks and stops
 them spreading together)
5 pots of green and 5 pots of purple
 house leeks
John Innes No3 and multi-purpose compost
Horticultural grit

Plant care...

Sempervivums rarely need watering. Only if the compost completely dries out for a long time and the plants shrivel, or the smaller rosettes close, should you give them a drink. Being too wet is far more damaging for them. So plant in a free-draining mix of John Innes No3, multi-purpose compost and horticultural grit mixed in equal parts. In wet autumns and winters move pots to a sheltered place where they will be protected from the rain.

1. Cover the holes in the base of the pot with stones and fill with the compost mix.

2. Put the smaller pot into the larger one, sinking it into the compost until the pot rims are level. Then fill with compost up to 1cm from the top of the pots.

3. Knock the house leeks out of their pots and gently tear them apart into individual rosettes.

4. Plant the green house leeks in the round pot and the purple outside by making a hole with your finger, lowering the roots into it and firming the compost down around them. Position in a sunny spot.

Training Wires for Climbers

A framework of wires running up a wall creates a ladder for climbers such as passion-flower and roses to scramble up, and also enables fruit trees and roses to be trained. Using long screws with hooked tops (vine eyes) to hold the wire proud of the wall creates more space for plants to grow and for air to circulate behind their stems. The free movement of air is particularly important when training roses, fruit trees or growing clematis as it prevents the build-up of fungal diseases, including powdery mildew and blackspot, which thrive in airless conditions.

If you think that a wire framework like this looks excessive, especially next to newly planted climbers, rest assured that it's worth the effort. It's very time-consuming to untangle a large climber from a too-small support that has come away from the wall, and, once established, climbing plants grow quickly and cover large areas.

You will need...

10cm vine eyes, enough for rows 60cm apart
 with 2m between the eyes in a row
Blocks of wood to support the end vine eyes
Bolt tensioners, 2 per wire support
2mm plastic-coated wire
Rawlplugs

1. Depending on the ultimate size and spread of your climber, drill holes in the wall, starting 60cm from the ground for vine eyes to be screwed into. Allow 60cm gaps between the rows and 2m intervals between vine eyes in the same row. Push Rawlplugs in the holes.

2. Screw in all the vine eyes except those at either end of the wall.

3. The tension in the wire often bends the end vine eyes over. To prevent this, drill through a block of wood the same length of the vine eye shank (the distance from the bottom of the eye to the start of the thread) and push the vine eye through this before screwing to the wall.

4. Cut the wire to length and thread it through the vine eyes. Tie the ends to bolt tensioners – bolts with a hook or eye at one end with a long screw thread with a nut and washer at the other.

5. Then slide the bolt through the end vine eye, put on the washer and tighten the nut with a spanner. The wire is tight when there are no dips or kinks in it.

6. Climbers such as clematis and passion-flower benefit from extra vertical wires, which make their climb up the wall easier. Tie the wire to the top and bottom horizontals, wrapping once around each of the horizontals between. Space 60cm apart to make equal squares along the wall.

Spending as much time as possibl

ut of doors is what summer is all about. Whether it's to play, work, eat or drink, everything is best done outside.

For children, the garden offers limitless opportunities for play, and there's plenty of wildlife to discover.

Relaxing to the gentle burble of running water on hot days is the name of the game, being mesmerised as it dances and splashes down a waterfall.

In summer everyone wants flowers, and pots and patios are the places to display cascades of bedding plants covered in blooms. More subtle flowers also appear, such as ornamental grasses with their barley straw stems reflecting the sunshine.

Even after the sun has gone down the temperature is still warm. With a few garden lights and candles, parties can go on well into the night.

Summer

Ridge Tile Waterfall

You might think that creating a waterfall in your garden would be a major task, one usually left to landscapers. Yet a modern and simple way of creating a cascade can be achieved with ridge tiles – those traditionally used to cover the apex of a roof. The beauty of using this material is that it removes a great deal of the work and skill required to build a natural-looking rock cascade, and you don't even need to use cement to fix them. As with all man-made waterfalls, a water source is unnecessary. Once the pond is filled, the water is recycled on a loop, starting in the pond, then pumped to the top of the gradient, only to cascade back down, creating movement and a pleasing patter as it descends.

Unlike natural stone features this cascade will never look out of place in an urban city garden. Because it can be as short or long as you like it is ideal for small gardens.

You will need...

1,500 litres-per-hour low-voltage pond pump
4m of hose (compatible in size to the pump)
1 3m x 2.5m pond liner
3m x 2.5m of pond liner-underlay/old carpet
5 terracotta ridge tiles
Terracotta urn
Spade
Stanley knife
5 bags of pebbles

1. Dig out a hole for the pond. This can be as large as you want but the one featured here is 1.2m across and 50cm deep. Pile the soil up into a ramp on one side of the hole, with a gully running up its centre.

2. Cover the pond with underlay and pond liner and run the pump hose from the pond up to the top of the gully. Then line the gully, making sure that the liner drapes into the pond to catch any leaks.

3. Push the hose at the top of the gully through the hole in the bottom of the urn.

4. Lay the ridge tiles up the centre of the gully, each over-lapping the one below by 2–3cm – work up from the bottom. Position the bottom tile so that it juts out over the edge of the pond to create a good fall of water, finishing off with the top tile sitting under the lip of the urn to catch the water. Ensure the base of each tile slopes towards the pond.

5. Adjust the tiles until you are happy with how they look and pack soil around them to hold them firm. Disguise the edges of the liner with more soil.

6. Fix the pump to the hose, fill the pond with water and check the waterfall for leaks. Make any adjustments to the position of the urn or tiles as necessary, then line the pond with pebbles and plant up around it.

Copper Wall Fountain

Of the many effects water creates, one of my favourites is when it races over the top of a weir. As the water swells to pass, the surface becomes an unbroken fast-flowing and shimmering blade. While the play of most water features is limited to jets and fountains, this modern copper trough directs the course into a sheet of water. Because it's fixed to a wall, it suits tiny spaces and, being raised up, it's on view from indoors. I have my fountain at the end of an alley that runs down the side of my house and when I open my office window the sound of the cascade fills the whole room.

You will need...

0.2cm x 60cm x 120cm sheet of copper
 (it comes in standard sizes)
1cm x 60cm x 120cm sheet
 of marine plywood
Marker pen
Jigsaw with sheet metal blade and
 wood-cutting blade
Mallet
Metal File Pliers
Wood screws and wall plugs
90cm of hosepipe
600 litres-per-hour pond pump
60cm of 30mm x 50mm wooden batten
1m of pond liner
Silicone glue and glue gun
Copper tacks

Cutting Plan...

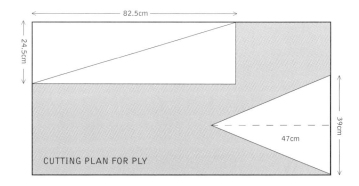

CUTTING PLAN FOR PLY

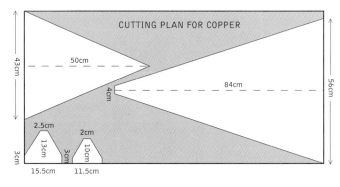

CUTTING PLAN FOR COPPER

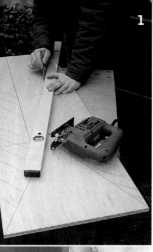

1. Mark out and cut the marine ply according to the cutting plan.

2. If necessary, hammer out any creases in the copper with a rubber mallet. Mark out and cut the copper according to the plan using a jigsaw fitted with a sheet metal-cutting blade.

3. File the edges of the copper to remove any sharp burrs. When the wood is placed on the copper, there should be a 1.5cm flap of copper all the way round the edge.

4. Make a 90 degree fold in the larger copper triangle by leaning it half over the edge of a table and gently beating it down with the rubber mallet.

Continued over >

Such a contemporary feature can command a high price-tag in a shop, but follow the steps below and you'll find it's economical and straightforward to make and that the copper is easy to work. Over time, the copper will weather to a verdigris green, or you can keep it clean with metal polish to maintain that fresh, designer look.

5. Position the two longest edges of the triangle 1cm out over the edge of a table and bend these to over 90 degrees to make flaps at either side.

6. Drill and fix the two wooden triangles to the wall leaving a 1.5cm gap between them.

7. Drill a hole two-thirds of the way up from the base in the larger copper triangle; make it just large enough for a hosepipe to pass through. Push one end of the hosepipe 2cm through the hole, sit the copper onto the wooden triangles running the hose down the gap between them. Hammer copper tacks through the copper flaps to hold in place.

8. Put the last plywood triangle in place and sit two 20cm lengths of wooden batten on top, sitting them against the walls. Mark their positions then fix with screws to the walls and screw the plywood triangle to them.

9. When in place, line with pond liner and put the pond pump in. Cut the hose to length and fix to the pump.

10. Put the bottom copper triangle in position and tuck the wire for the pump down the side. Fix with copper tacks hammered in down the edges next to the wall, away from the pond liner.

11. Cut two triangles of copper with 1cm flaps. Sit them on an angular off-cut of plywood and bend over the flaps 45 degrees using a rubber hammer.

12. Position the larger triangle just below the hose and 1cm in from the edges. Fix in place with copper tacks.

13. Run a bead of clear silicone sealer along the inside edges of the triangle and smear with a wet finger to fill any gaps. Glue around the hosepipe to seal it and along the flaps of the smaller triangle. Position this triangle over the end of the hose with its bottom edge resting on a piece of plywood until the glue is dry.

14. Fill the sump with water and turn on the pump. Add more silicone to plug any leaks and bend the flap at the top of the waterfall until you have a smooth splash-free blade of water.

Hurricane Lights

Finished look... Hang the jars against a sheltered wall for a striking effect and to create a brighter, useful light source.

Sitting out on a warm summer night in a garden lit by the stars and candlelight alone is a magical experience. The garden appears exotic as familiar garden features such as trees, patios and eating tables are transformed by the flickering orange of the candles. By using recycled glass jars and glass paints bought from art shops, you can make your own candle-lit hurricane lights. These are so simple to make, even children can have a go. If you're after a chic, classy look, keep your designs to just two or three colours, or you can make the lights bright and fun by incorporating all the colours of the rainbow. And of course the lights look just as good on a window-sill to welcome visitors during the festive season.

You will need...

Glass jars
Copper wire
Tea candles
Artist's paint brush
Transparent glass paint
Tube of silver contour-lining paste
Pliers

Scented citronella...

Candlelight isn't simply atmospheric: if scented citronella candles are burned, midges and mosquitoes can be kept at bay. Citronella is distilled from a South Asian variety of lemon-grass (Cymbopogon).

1. Paint the 'leaded' lines of the design with the contour-lining paste. The lines will be straighter and less wobbly if you sit the jar on the table and spin it slowly round with the nozzle of the tube touching the jar and the paste squeezing through it at an even rate.

2. Paint the squares with the coloured transparent glass paint. To get an even coat, load the brush and touch its tip on to the glass so the paint flows from it and spreads evenly across the square.

3. Cut a 30cm length of copper wire and twist a loop in it 10cm from one end. Then wrap the wire around the top of the jar, twisting the two ends until tight. Cut the short end off, bend the long piece over the top of the jar, and attach to the hook to make a handle.

Monster Footprints

Imagine you were a child again and you found a set of giant footprints in the garden. The sense of excitement and adventure would be enormous! Even when you realised that they weren't real, they would still form the basis of exciting games, such as chasing imaginary monsters or playing hopscotch between the feet. Gardens are fantastic places for children to develop their imaginations, even more so if you add a feature like these. The feet could be made to run between dens, or to form the basis of a 'jungle' path out of adult sight along the back of a border. More practically, they could be stepping stones bridging a muddy patch of lawn or leading to the washing line.

You will need...

50cm x 75cm sheet of timber
Jigsaw
Ballast (approximately half a bag per monster foot)
Cement
Trowel and bucket
Pebbles for toes
Masonry paint

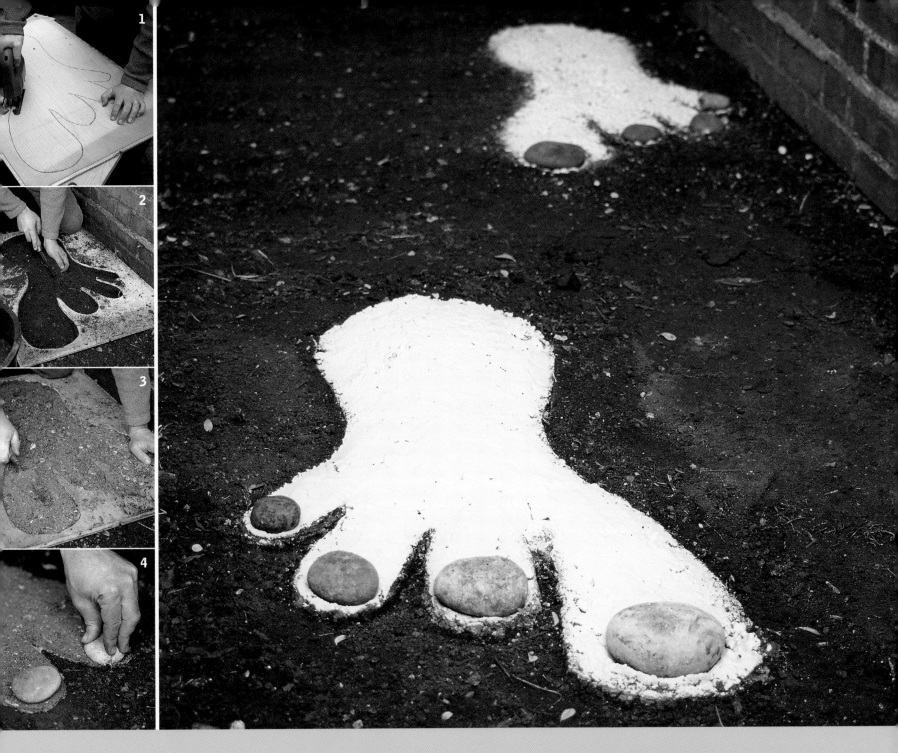

1. Make a pattern by drawing the shape of a monster footprint on the timber sheet; cut it out using a jigsaw.

2. Put the sheet on the ground and dig out the soil to a depth of 5cm, making sure the soil around the sides of the foot follows the foot pattern exactly.

3. Make a concrete mix containing 1 part cement to 6 parts ballast, pour into the hole and smooth flat with a trowel.

4. Remove the pattern and push pebbles into the concrete at the ends of the toes to make nails and leave to dry. Then paint with brightly coloured masonry paint.

Valentine Apples

A Valentine Apple is a simple but extremely effective idea which works on the same principles as blanching. Light levels are manipulated to ripen one area of a fruit more than another by wrapping them up to block out the light. Although I've created a heart, you could just as easily have a flower or a loved one's initials. All you need is access to a fruit tree, some weed-suppressing membrane and a good measure of patience.

For a romantic gift ready for Valentine's Day in February, I chose a variety of apple tree called 'Sturmer Pippin'. This produces fruit that ripens early in the new year and can be kept in a cool place until the right time. But any tree with red or blush fruit is suitable. As Valentine's gifts go, you'd be hard pressed to find one more unique, economical or showing such patient dedication.

You will need...

20cm squares of weed-suppressing
membrane sheet
Stapler and scissors

1. Wait until the fruit is nearly full-size but still green. Cut out a heart shape in the middle of the weed-suppressing membrane sheet. Then select apples on the sunniest side of the tree that are free from blemishes and bird damage. Remove any leaves that shadow their skin from the sun.

2. Wrap the apples in the sheet with the heart facing towards the sun, bunching excess material around the stalk and the back. Bunching in this way excludes light from around the stalk and gives a little slack for the apple to grow into. Staple the sheet into position, taking care not to damage the apple.

3. It's a good idea to do more than one apple just in case your chosen apple gets damaged or falls from the tree prematurely.

4. Remove the membrane when the fruit is ripe and store in a cool, dark, well-ventilated shed.

Bamboo Trees

Finished look... Tufty grasses anchor the bamboo poles to the ground, playing up their exotic look and making them appear as though they are growing.

A simple sculpture can be created for a garden cheaply and easily from a display of out-sized bamboo poles. Play up their oriental look by combining with grasses or position with pebbles for a modern, minimalist effect. Whatever the style, they add instant height and become a focal point. They are ideal in small gardens as they cast no shade and take up little space. Children cannot resist weaving between the poles and they relieve treasured garden trees from that duty. For a child's garden, simply knock them into a lawn or a soft bark chipping play surface. Construction is easy and quick and the bamboo poles are now widely available from garden centres. Buy steel fence spikes or tubing from hardware stores.

You will need...

10cm x 2.5m bamboo poles
Club hammer
1.2m metal fence spikes/steel tubing

Big bamboo...

The large bamboo poles sold in garden centres in the UK are imported from Vietnam and China. They are harvested from the Giant Chinese Moso bamboo (Phyllostacys pubescens) that grows 26m tall and up to 30cm in diameter. Theses immense poles have long been used in the construction industry and for furniture manufacture, while the cooked tender young shoots are considered a delicacy.

1. Hammer the fence spikes about 60cm into the ground with the lump hammer until they are firm. If you don't have fence spikes, 1-inch steel tubing is just as good. Make each spike lean over at a slightly different angle to make them look more natural.

2. The inside of the bamboo is made of compartments separated by thin walls of wood, which have to be broken so the pole will slide over the metal spikes.

3. To do this, raise the bamboo pole above a fence spike and ram it down onto it, breaking through the compartment walls until the bottom of the bamboo pole sits on the ground.

Urn Water Feature

This little feature is very simple to make and would be equally at home on a patio or in a conservatory or porch. Because it is small and self-contained, it can easily be moved, so wherever you sit, you can always hear the sound of gently splashing water to help you relax.

Although only a small feature, it will still attract wildlife. The one in my garden is visited by thirsty butterflies that prefer the easily accessible water running over the pebbles to the more hazardous open water in the pond.

You will need...

60cm terracotta pan
Terracotta urn
600 litres-per-hour low-voltage pond pump
1 square metre of pond liner
60cm of hosepipe
2 house bricks
60cm x 60cm of fine galvanised mesh
Bag of pebbles
Floristry beads – blue and green
Tin snips or old scissors
Drill with 12mm masonry bit (if the hole
 in the urn needs to be enlarged)

Pond pump care...

Because the water feature is small, the water will need to be topped up regularly especially in hot and windy weather to prevent the pump running dry. You'll know when the water level is low as the pump sounds as though it's labouring. In winter, remove and wash the pump and its filter under the tap and store in a frost-free place.

1. Position the pan where you want the fountain to go and spread the pond liner inside it.

2. Push the hosepipe onto the outlet of the pump. (To make the rubber softer and easier to stretch, dip the end of the hose in hot water first.)

3. Put the pump in the bottom of the pan and place two house bricks either side of it to make a platform for the urn to sit on.

4. Fill with water and trim the edge of the pond liner level with the rim of the pan. Then cut the mesh to fit inside the rim of the pan and position on top of the bricks.

5. Rest the urn on the mesh and push the end of the hose through the drainage hole in its base. Enlarge the hole by redrilling it with a 12mm masonry bit if necessary.

6. Cover the mesh with pebbles and scatter floristry beads between them to add colour.

Globe Fountain

Not that long ago, creating water features was an arduous task. But with the advent of a wider range of pond pumps and accessories suited to smaller features, it's now quick and easy, and the possibilities for creativity when making water displays are endless. This ceramic and glass fountain brings together materials easily found in garden centres and chosen for the way they emphasise the shiny, sparkling nature of the water. Because it's small, it suits patio and balcony gardeners and wouldn't look out of place in a conservatory.

You will need...

600 litres-per-hour pond pump with a
 fountain attachment kit
1 square metre of plastic pond liner
Drill and a selection of masonry bits
 ranging in size from 3mm–12mm
Plastic gaffer tape/electrical tape
Large terracotta pot
25cm–30cm wide glazed terracotta globe
2 house bricks
30cm of hosepipe
60cm x 60cm of galvanised wire mesh
Tin snips or old kitchen scissors
Bag of pebbles
Glass chippings or glass floristry beads

Drilling holes in pottery...

To drill a hole in a terracotta or glazed pot you need a drill, a selection of masonry drill bits ranging from 3mm–12mm and plastic tape. First, stick the tape over the spot where you want the hole to be and then drill with the smallest bit in the chuck. Take your time, exerting only light pressure on the drill to reduce the risk of smashing through the pot as the terracotta gets thinner. Once you've made a hole with the smallest bit, widen it by drilling with the larger bits, working up in size until the hole is the required diameter.

1. Drill a hole the same width as the fountain extension tube in the top of the globe.

2. Push the hosepipe onto one end of the fountain attachment tube and push the other end into the drilled hole from inside the pot until it is held firmly in position. If it's too tight, pare down the end with sandpaper, and if it's too loose wrap gaffer tape around the end.

3. Line the inside of the pot with the plastic liner.

4. Put the pump in the bottom and position house bricks either side of it, making a platform for the globe to sit on that is 1–2cm lower than the rim of the pot.

5. Fill with water and trim the edge of the pond liner level with the rim of the pot. Then cut the galvanised mesh with tin snips or an old pair of scissors so that it fits just inside the rim of the pot. Cut a hole in the centre of the mesh large enough for the hosepipe to go through.

6. Pass the end of the hosepipe through the mesh and fix it onto the pump. If the fit is too tight, soften the rubber in the hose and make it more stretchy by dipping the end in water just off the boil and greasing the inside with petroleum jelly. Sit the globe on the bricks in the middle of the pot and fill the pot with water. Cover the mesh with pebbles and glass chippings and top up with water regularly to stop the pump from running dry.

Barrel Ponds

Creating a pond in a barrel isn't a new idea but what makes this project different is the sheer size of the barrel – at least three times as big as the average barrel pond! It makes much more of an impact without taking up much more space so it's ideal for patio gardens. Because the volume of water is greater, more plants can be grown and it's less likely to gather algae than the small bucket-sized equivalents.

Adding a barrel pond to your garden will give it a whole new dimension. The water itself provides reflections and movement, particularly if a mini fountain is installed, and fish will live happily in it. Even without fish it will be a focus for wildlife, with butterflies stopping to drink the water and even dragonflies buzzing around it.

You will need...

Dwarf pond plants
1m half-barrel without drainage holes
Spirit level
House bricks
8–10 1L black plastic pots
Aquatic compost
Gravel

Buying barrels

Half-barrels have exotic pasts: they start their lives in Spain as sherry casks and are then used as whisk(e)y barrels in Ireland and Scotland, where the traces of sherry help to flavour the whisk(e)y. Finally they are cut in half and sold at garden centres. When buying, look out for the name of a château or distillery branded on the base and charring on the inside. These indicate that the barrel is authentic and watertight, as copies made from ordinary planks, which are common in garden centres, are not. If unsure, check with garden centre staff before you buy.

1. Choose an open sunny site for the pond and roll the barrel into position. Be sure that you're happy with its location as it can't be moved once filled with water.

2. Check that its top is flat with a spirit level and build up the sides with wedges of wood or slate if necessary.

3. Fill the barrel with water. If it leaks, it's because the timbers have dried out and shrunk. But if you keep it topped up, the wood will expand and naturally plug the gaps.

Continued over >

Choosing pond plants

Pond plants are divided into different types according to where they grow in the pond. Marginals grow around the edges; deep water plants, such as water lilies, root on the bottom; and oxygenators float in the water. The key to success when choosing plants for barrel ponds is picking those that don't grow too quickly and won't swamp their neighbours.

The following is a selection of plants that work well...

Oxygenators... Hornwort (Ceratophyllum demersum) with whorls of dark green foliage in summer.

Deep water plants... Dwarf water lilies, including the slow-growing pygmy forms such as white fragrantly scented Nymphaea pygmaea 'Odorata Minor'

Marginals... Corkscrew rush (Juncus effusus 'Spiralis') with spiralling evergreen stems; miniature bulrush (Typha minima) with chocolate-brown drumstick-like flowers; and Japanese Water Iris (Iris ensata) with 5in flowers of white, blue or pink.

4. Plant up the marginal plants in 8–10 1L black plastic pots using aquatic compost. Cover the surface of the pots with gravel to stop the compost floating up and clouding the water.

5. The oxygenating plants can be placed straight into the water, but the marginal plants need to sit on shelves. Make these by lowering black plastic pots upside down into the water. Then sit the planted pots of marginals on top.

6. Water Lilies like to grow in deep water but cannot cope with the low light levels until their leaf stalks are long enough to reach the surface of the water. To encourage the leaf stalks to grow, make a stack of bricks from the base of the barrel to 15cm below the water's surface.

7. Lower the Water Lily onto the bricks and, as the leaf stalks grow in length, remove the bricks layer by layer until the lily pot sits on the base of the barrel. Trim back any plants that threaten to crowd out their neighbours.

Barrel Sand-pit

Tip... The best thing about this sand-pit is that the doors can be closed on any mess left by children and – hey presto! – your garden is tidy.

Children and immaculate gardens are two things that generally don't go together. But because this self-contained barrel doubles as a sand-pit and a place to store toys, your garden can still look stylish. Painted up with bright enticing colours to attract curious little hands, or camouflaged to blend into a border, the barrel lid will also keep the sand clean, dry and free from fouling cats. Older children can be involved in making or decorating the barrel and once outgrown it can be converted to a water feature or a planter.

You will need...

1m half-barrel
Half a sheet (120cm x 120cm) of
 12mm marine plywood
Jigsaw
Work bench
Electric sander or a thick layer of
 weed-suppressing membrane and
 1cm galvanised felt tacks
Drill and screwdriver
4 20cm gate hinges
50mm screws
10mm screws
Light and dark blue outdoor wood-stain
4–5 bags of play sand

Safe and sound...

It's a good idea to have finger-holes in the doors so that they can be secured open when the children are playing. Thread lengths of rope through the finger-holes and tie them to 1m wooden stakes hammered into the soil on either side of the barrel. The stakes will also take undue stress off the hinges.

1. Using an electric sander, remove any sharp edges from the inside of the barrel. If you don't have a sander, line the inside of the barrel with a thick layer of weed-suppressing membrane and fix in place with 1cm galvanised felt tacks.

2. Lay the plywood sheet on the ground. Place the barrel on top and draw around it with a thick pencil. Then mark a line on the plywood and the side of the barrel so that the two can be matched up easily later on.

3. Put the plywood on a work bench and cut out the circle with a jigsaw. Then cut the circle in half to make the doors and, at its widest point, cut a 12cm strip off the side of each door. This allows the doors to be hinged.

4. Lay the cut plywood on the top of the barrel, leaving 1mm gaps between each piece of wood. Fix the two 12cm strips to the barrel with 50mm screws and the doors to these with gate hinges. Check for sharp edges and sand off if necessary.

5. Dig a hole big enough to house the base of the barrel, backing up the spoil behind it. Paint blue stripes on the doors with wood stain and fill with play sand.

Sleepy Hollow

For a light... Position the trunk over a single outdoor spotlight fitted with a coloured bulb.

A tree trunk in its natural state has an inherent beauty, capable of adding a richness and a sense of timelessness to a garden. But stumps and forked branches are often seen as inconvenient, having little use outdoors for edging and hard to dispose of through a chipper. Yet wood like this can be hollowed out to enhance its character and transform it into a wooden cylinder that can be planted up or wired up for atmospheric lighting. Traditionally ferns have been planted into logs to make a miniature woodland scene, but if you fancy something different, use grassy-leaved plants to contrast with the wood of the log.

Hollowing out is easy with the right bits and a powerful drill, and if you don't own one, they are cheap to rent from tool hire shops. Tip... If there are no knots or they are unevenly distributed on the trunk, draw on your own, locating them in recesses to create a natural look. Then drill and chisel out (as opposite) until the trunk is hollow.

You will need...

Timber
Wood chisels
Mallet
Drill and auger bit

Plants...

Use drought-tolerant grasses such as blue fescue (Festuca glauca), sedges like Carex 'Frosted Curls' and black lily turf (Ophiopogon planiscapus 'Nigrescens').

1. Starting at the ends of the stump, drill out as much heartwood as possible to the depth of the drill bit

2. What you cannot drill out, remove by chiselling: the more holes you can drill, the easier this is to do.

3. Once the end holes are too deep to chisel out comfortably, drill in from the sides through knots and natural cracks in the trunk. Then chisel out the remaining wood

as before. If there are no knots or they are unevenly distributed on the trunk, draw on your own, locating them in recesses or creases to create a natural look. Then drill and chisel out as before until the trunk is hollow.

4. Position the trunk where you want it to go and fill with compost. Then plant up with grasses, ferns or bedding plants.

Clay Pipe Planters

Cutting clay pipes by hand
1. Dig over a patch of soil to make it soft and fluffy. Lay the pipe onto it and mark a line with chalk or a stone around where you want to cut. Then put the blade of the bolster on the line and gently hammer.

2. Rotate the pipe between blows on the bolster, working your way along the line. Keep hitting and rotating. Eventually, the tone of the pipe as it's hit will change and it will fracture in two.

Clay pipes make stylish planters for dotting among border plants or for clustering in groups to give a modern 'mini-skyscraper' look. The shades and texture of clay are as rich as any terracotta pot bought from the garden centre and if you are the type of gardener who neglects to water pots regularly, they are more forgiving. This is because the soil that fills them is not separated from the soil in the border, so water is soaked up by the roots.

Pipes come in many shapes and sizes but bear in mind, the taller the pipe, the thirstier the plants will be, as they are further from the water in the soil. Many different plants will grow in them happily but ornamental grasses look the best as their floppy tufts of leaves contrast with the clean straight sides of the pipes while the soft muted colours of the leaves complement their biscuit and terracotta shades.

The place to buy is a builders' merchants. Look out for any with broken or cracked ends, as they're no use to builders but ideal for your purposes and will often be sold cheaply. (See left for tips on cutting and cleaning up their ends.)

You will need...

Clay pipes over 20cm in diameter
Spade
Multi-purpose compost
Plastic liner

Grasses – Carex 'Frosted Curls', Festuca glauca, Millium effusum 'Aureum', Carex stricta, Molinia 'Variegata'
Club hammer
Bolster and safety goggles for cutting pipes

1. Bury the pipes 20cm into the soil for stability and to ensure that the plants can draw up moisture from below ground level.

2. Line each pipe with plastic – cut-up compost bags will do – to reduce water loss.

3. Fill each pipe with a 50/50 mix of multi-purpose compost and good garden soil. The soil holds the moisture and the compost keeps the texture of the soil open and airy.

4. Plant the grasses in the top leaving 3cm between the rim of the pipe and the top of the soil. Water in well and keep watered during dry spells.

Wooden Planters

I have used large wooden planters to grow everything from ornamental grasses to grapevines. They are the ideal solution for soil-less gardens and patios, allowing groups of plants to be grown together just like in a border. Unlike the alternative of lots of small pots, they require less regular watering and are inexpensive to make.

Wooden planters have advantages over other materials as they insulate the roots from drought and cold weather. Incredibly simple to make, they can be cut to fit any space but a good tip to remember is the larger they are, the less quickly they dry out.

There are lots of ways you can decorate them, from paint effects, such as stencilling and distressing, to gluing on shells and glass beads.

You will need...

8m of 15cm x 1.5cm timber plank*
Wood saw
1.3m of 50mm triangular batten
Garden wood stain
Drill
12 50mm screws
Compost and plants such as euphorbias,
 cineraria, petunias and osteospermum

* Makes a 100cm x 30cm x 30cm planter

1. The first job is to measure and cut the timber planks into six 1m lengths for the sides and base, and four 33cm lengths for the ends. Then cut four 25cm lengths of the triangular batten for the corners. When all of the wood is cut, it should look like figure 1 (*see* opposite) when laid out.

2. To make the sides of the planter, lay two 1m planks side by side with a length of triangular batten on top at each end and screw in place.

3. Then screw on the two ends of the planter, taking care to keep the top of the planks level.

4. To make the bottom, fix the two remaining planks in position by screwing to short lengths of batten as shown.

5. Drill drainage holes in the base so that excess water can escape. The larger the holes the better, as they're less likely to get blocked up by compost. You'll need to drill one hole for every 30cm along the base of the box.

6. Paint the box with protective wood stain. Move it into the garden, fill with compost and plant up. For this scheme I used euphorbias at the back, silver cineraria in the middle and petunais and osteospermum at the front.

Autumn is one of the most productiv

mes in the garden, which is brimming with things to harvest and use – from fallen leaves to the last of the summer pumpkins.

It is a time for eking out the summer and extending crops, as well as welcoming in the winter. The earth is ripe for planting and more pleasant to work than at any other time of year, holding the warmth of summer but softened by rain and easy to dig.

The daylight, although diminishing noticeably, has a magical quality, highlighting the rich colours of stone and terracotta, which in turn contrast with the warm reds and yellows of ripening berries and the flame shades of fallen leaves.

Autumn

Mosaic Star Stepping Stone

It's the detail that makes a garden beautiful, and mosaics are definitely one of those details that add a touch of individuality. They needn't be confined to walls and furniture: this stepping stone can be used at the crossroads between pathways or as a full stop to a walkway. You could even link a number of paths with a series of stepping stone mosaics, perhaps developing the theme to include other celestial motifs such as the moon, planets or even figures of the zodiac.

You will need...

Spade
10 house bricks
Bag of cement
4 bags of sharp sand
13 12cm terracotta floor tiles
13 12cm biscuit-coloured ceramic tiles
Builder's trowel and bucket
Hammer
5 nails and string line
Rubber grouting blade

Cement made simple...

It's not always necessary to add water to cement and sharp sand to make the mix go off. Water in the air or from the soil will be enough to start the hardening process. The reason you add water is to create smooth, level surfaces and to make the mix sticky, which helps when laying small mosaic tiles.

1. You may need to cut the bricks to create an even curve. Put the brick on its edge on a bed of sand, placing a bolster where you want to cut and hammering sharply once. Turn it onto its opposite edge and repeat until it splits in two.

2. If you're making the mosaic in a path, lift out a paving slab and dig a hole 10cm deep and 1m wide in the soil. Flatten the base of the hole.

3. Make a 5:1 dry mix of sharp sand and cement and half fill the depth of the hole with it. Arrange the bricks in a circle burying them down in the mix and keeping them level. Leave overnight to dry.

4. Mix up another 5:1 sharp sand and cement mix – this time with water. Place this around the outside of the circle and smooth down to 1cm from the tops of the bricks. Then fill the centre of the circle smoothing to a level 2cm down from the top of the bricks.

Continued over >

Built properly, a mosaic stepping stone is a permanent feature that will grace your garden for a long time, provided you choose unglazed tiles made of stone, coloured clay or terracotta. These are best because they are frost-resistant, so their colour won't chip off in freezing weather, and they look more natural than brightly glazed tiles. An edging is necessary to stop the outside tiles from being dislodged. These should be chosen according to the colour of the tiles in the mosaic and the existing materials in your garden. As well as bricks, granite setts, pavers and slate all make attractive surrounds.

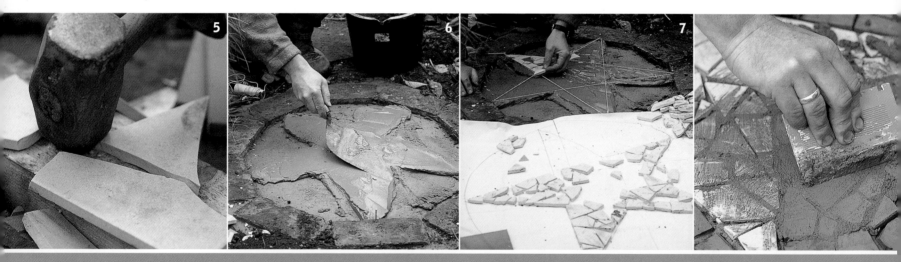

5. Break up the tiles into chunks. Sketch out a full-size drawing of the star and fit the pieces of tile onto it with 2–3mm joints between them.

6. Make a wet 3:1 sharp sand and cement mix and arrange into a rough star that's level with the tops of the bricks at the centre, but slopes gradually down to 0.5cm from their tops at the edges.

7. Hammer a nail into the concrete just inside the brick edges at the points of the star and run string guidelines between them. Put the biscuit-coloured tiles into position first, keeping an eye on the levels so that the star slopes out evenly from the its centre to the tops of the brick edges. Once the star is completed, leave for an hour to firm up and fill in the gaps between the points with 3:1 sharp sand and cement. Lay the terracotta tiles onto it and leave overnight to dry.

8. Use a grouting blade to fill the gaps between the tiles with a moist 3:1 mix of sharp sand and cement. Leave to dry for two hours and wipe over with a damp cloth.

Trompe l'Oeil Door

A trompe l'oeil is a deceptive feature, the French phrase literally meaning to 'fool the eye'. It's a centuries-old technique that dates back to pre-Roman times, with ancient examples surviving at Pompeii and Eurculaneum. By altering the perspective, an illusion is created, perhaps making a garden look longer than in reality or depicting a lifelike feature such as a window that isn't really there. In a garden the effect adds surprise, mystery and whimsical character while being a practical way of disguising ugly walls or distant eyesores.

Using mirrors in a trompe l'oeil enhances the deception, bringing light into a dark place and reversing the image of nearby features, thus making familiar views unfamiliar. Mirrors can be bought cheaply from second-hand furniture stores and cut to size by your local glazier.

You will need*...

1,200mm x 2,400mm x 12mm sheet
 of marine plywood
3 old wardrobe mirrors
Pot of bitumastic paint
Jigsaw/circular saw
Drill
Screwdrivers
70 20mm screws
1m of fibre board
10mm tacks

5m of 50mm x 100mm timber
15 70mm screws
5 1,800mm x 150mm feathered fence boards
String line
2 colours of green paint
Door bolt

* Makes a doorway 180cm tall and 1m wide

1. Buy three wardrobe mirrors, preferably without bevelled edges. Coat the reverse side with bitumastic paint to prevent moisture damage.

2. Lay the mirrors onto the plywood, marking a rectangular border around them that is 50mm wide along the bottom and 80mm wide around the top and sides.

3. Cut off excess plywood outside the rectangle and use to box around the mirrors. Fix in place with 20mm screws.

4. Fill in the centre space between the mirrors with the remainder of the plywood.

Continued over >

For a simple trompe l'oeil, any mirror can be successfully placed in a garden setting, provided that its back and edges are protected with bitumastic paint. You only need a small piece of mirror showing to create the illusion, and this safeguards against birds flying into it. Blend mirrors into the garden by disguising edges with evergreen foliage – ivy is excellent – and by angling slightly to stop you seeing your reflection as you approach. Always place a mirror where you might expect to see a window, moon gate (see page 86) or door in a boundary.

5. To stop the mirrors from rattling and falling one behind the other, they have to sit at the same level as the marine ply 'boxing'. To do this, remove the mirrors and build up the levels with squares of fibreboard and tack into place.

6. Make the door frame from 50mm x 100mm timber and fix around the door with screws. You will need a top piece and two uprights for the sides. Make sure the door frame covers the outside edge of the mirrors to hold them in.

7. Put four uncut feather boards over the door area to help you visualise what the finished door will look like, and then, to create the illusion that the door is ajar, make a string triangle running from the top and bottom of the door to a peg 5m away. Position the peg two thirds up from the bottom of the door.

8. Once you're happy that the perspective looks right, remove the feather boards and cut them so that they decrease in size and look like the door is open. So cut a 40mm strip off the first board, a 50mm strips of the second, 60mm from the third and 70mm from the fourth. Arrange all the strips (and off-cuts) in order of size back in the door with the thickest next to the frame. Mark where the string crosses and cut to length.

9. To make running boards (the horizontals on a door), cut a feather board into three 60cm lengths and lay them on the door. Run a string line from the peg to the inside corner of each running board and mark with a pencil where the line crosses. Then saw to the line.

Tip... To enhance the illusion, create a false path with stepping stones leading up to it, positioning the stones so that they are reflected in the bottom mirror leading the eye beyond the door. The gravel path not only heightens the illusion but, more practically, prevents mud being splashed up onto the base of the mirror and hides the timber boxing that holds it in place.

10

10. Screw the slats and the running boards into place and your finished trompe l'oeil door will look like this, with the plywood frame housing the mirrors, which in turn are overlaid with your feather board 'door' (a simple door bolt will add to the effect). Move the door to its place in the garden and paint the timber with protective wood stain.

Wirework Urn

Wirework has been used in gardens since Victorian times but modern garden designers have recently brought it back into fashion using it to make containers and sculpture. Although the wire used in its construction is cheap, the price of finished pots and urns in garden centres can be prohibitive because of the craft needed to transform what is an unpromising raw material into something with symmetry, strength and beauty.

You can make your own, however, by following the technique shown below. The trick is to start by making a perfectly even frame and then working methodically and evenly. The result is a unique piece of wire sculpture for a fraction of the cost of a shop-bought version.

You will need*...

20m of 2mm galvanised wire
10m of 1mm galvanised wire
4m of 3mm galvanised wire
2 3L plastic pots
Sticky tape
2 pliers
Stanley knife

* Makes an urn 30cm tall and 30cm wide at the rim

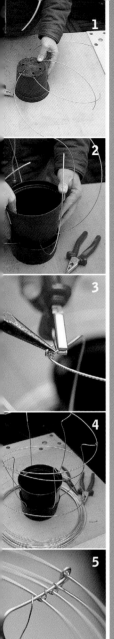

1. To make the frame of the urn, cut three 90cm lengths of the 3mm wire and thread through the drainage holes of a plastic pot, poking the ends in one side and drawing them out of the opposite hole. Make sure each of the six ends is exactly the same length.

2. Push the pot with the wires running through it down into another plastic pot that has had the top two-thirds cut off. The wires will bend in as the pots push together. When in as far as possible, hold in place with sticky tape.

3. Bend the wire ends outwards to make a symmetrical cup shape. Then bend each wire outwards again to form a gently sloping rim 12cm wide. As you go, check that all the wires are bent the same distance and in exactly the same place.

4. Put the roll of 2mm wire on a table with the pot frame inside. Lift the end of the roll to meet one of the ends of the frame and loop the two ends together with pliers. Repeat this on the other five 'uprights' of the frame to create the outer rim of the urn as shown.

5. Cut the 1mm wire into six 70cm lengths and tie to each of the loops on the rim as shown. Start coiling the 2mm wire around the frame, plaiting it to each upright with the 1mm wire. Leave 1cm gaps between each coil.

6. Work your way down taking care to keep the gaps between the wires the same and the overall shape of the urn symmetrical.

7. Cut the pots away with a Stanley knife to make working easier and finish the sides with the urn turned upside-down. For the base, spiral the wire into the centre tying in as before.

Cobble Roundel

Cobbles have an 'earth-born' look that enables them to be set against a host of other paving materials, such as brick, concrete and natural stone, without looking out of place or making the garden look bitty. They blend into any setting whether cottage, modern or Japanese in style and are useful for mulching borders, edging patios and for making cobbled paths. They also make beautiful roundels for pots or statues to stand on, or to accommodate a chair and drinks table amongst the foliage of plants in a border. When incorporated into the inside curve of a path, or at the junction where two paths cross, a cobble roundel will add detail and extra interest.

You will need*...

4 bags of 50–75mm cobbles
Spade
Bag of cement
3 bags of sharp sand
Gardening or builder's trowel
Club hammer
Short length of timber
Gloves
Hand-brush
Hand sprayer

* Makes an 80cm circle

1. Dig a circular hole 1m wide and 10–12cm deep. Level its base and firm the ground with the soles of your boots.

2. Pour two bags of sand and half the cement (roughly 4 parts sand to 1 cement) into a wheelbarrow and mix with a spade.

3. The mix is ready when it's an even grey colour, at which point it can be poured into the hole.

4. Smooth the sand–cement mix flat with a trowel or float. Wear gloves to do this as the cement is caustic.

5. Push the pebbles roughly half way into the mix point side up, building up in circles around one central pebble. Work your way to the edges of the roundel keeping the tops of the pebbles as level with each other as possible.

Continued over >

Cobbles are available in single and mixed colours ranging from black to pink, to speckled grey and white. Single colours are more expensive but you can keep the costs down by using them selectively, highlighting shapes and detail among cheaper mixed and grey cobbles. In a roundel, black cobbles can be used to write an initial or edge the circle for greater definition. They could also be used to link larger pebbled areas together. If laying large areas, work in one-metre sections, allowing the base to of each to dry before moving on to the next. This makes it easier to keep levels true and allows the joints to be filled at the same time.

6. Make sure the outside ring of pebbles is supported either by compacted soil or a haunch of concrete.

7. Run a length of timber over the pebbles to check for high spots, evening them out by hammering on the timber until level.

8. Mix the remaining bag of sand and cement (roughly a 3:1 mix) and brush between the pebbles, filling their joints about two-thirds of the way up.

9. Set the hand sprayer to a fine mist and wash off the tops of the pebbles. Leave for 48 hours to dry completely, before placing pots.

Ornamental Cloche

Tip... In autumn and spring, daytime temperatures can soar, causing plants beneath cloches to overheat and wilt. Prevent this by propping the lid open with a bamboo cane, allowing air to circulate.

Cloches extend the growing season of plants by shielding them from cold winter winds and trapping the heat from the sun. Modern cloches tend to put practicality and economy above ornament and can look out of place, while antique Victorian cloches are both useful and attractive but very expensive to buy.

However, you can replicate the mini-glass house style of the old cloches using perspex and piano hinges to achieve the same effect for far less expense.

You will need*...

90cm x 180cm sheet of perspex
1.2m of 20mm 'L'-shaped
 aluminium brackets
4.2m of 20mm aluminium piano hinges
120mm x 4mm set screws (mini
 bolts) and nuts
All-surface marker pen
Straight edge
Stanley knife with a scoring blade
100cm x 20cm wooden batten to
 support the perspex when drilling
Hacksaw/tin snips
Small file
Drill
Tape measure
Screwdriver

* Builds a 60cm x 60cm cloche that's 40cm tall

Cutting plan...

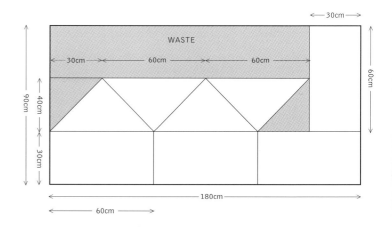

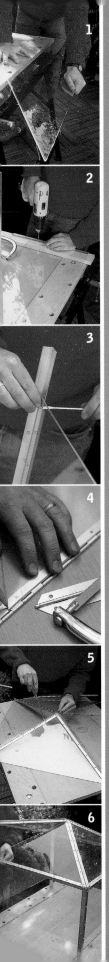

1. Mark out the cutting plan onto a sheet of perspex using an all-surface marker pen. Then put a straight edge along the lines and score twice with a Stanley knife. To snap the perspex, position it over the side of a table with the scored line running over the edge. With one hand holding the sheet flat to the table, snap the overhanging piece downwards in one quick movement.

2. Cut the aluminium 'L'-shaped bracket into four 40cm lengths with a hacksaw. Then, using the wooden batten for support, drill and screw the brackets onto each perspex side, leaving an overhang of 10cm to form the legs.

3. Join the sides together by drilling and fixing with set screws. Support the back of the perspex with the wooden batten when drilling and only tighten the set-screws 'finger tight' to prevent cracking.

4. Using a perspex roof section as a guide, measure the folded piano hinge against one of the shorter sides of the triangle and cut using a hacksaw or tin snips. Then file off any sharp edges. Repeat, making four lengths of hinge each with a bevelled edge, as shown.

5. Lay the roof sections on a flat surface leaving 1mm gaps between them. The gaps are essential, allow-ing the roof to be pulled up into a pyramid. Fix together with the four open piano hinges. Then cut and fix open lengths of hinge to the remaining sides of each roof section.

6. Pull the roof up into a pyramid and position on top of the base. Drill and fix three of the sides to the base with set screws, leaving one side as a flap for access. Take out to the garden and secure by pushing the legs into the soil.

Moon Gate

Firethorns or pyracanthas are hardworking shrubs. In spring they are covered with crowds of white flowers, followed by bright yellow, orange or red berries in autumn. Evergreen and adaptable, they cope in both shady and sunny spots and, left to their own devices, will mound up into plants the size of small trees. But with regular clipping their vigour is checked and they can be trained into topiary shapes or combined with trellis to make tight green topiary walls and arches.

When I first moved into my house, the centre of the garden was dominated by a huge pyracantha that had swamped a trellis screen. Normally, trellis screening makes an airy internal divide, but if covered by plants completely, it becomes as dark and oppressive as a fence. To remedy this, I cut a moon gate in the trellis, letting more light through and allowing tantalising glimpses of the garden beyond. Then I pruned and trained the pyracantha around the gate. Tip... If you don't have an internal boundary of trellis but want to recreate this project, it's easy. All you need to do is attach a square of trellis between two posts and plant two red-berried pyracanthas at the base and follow the instructions here.

You will need...

Trellis
Coping or small pruning saw
Chalk

String
Willow/dogwood stems
Gardening gloves

1. Unpruned shrubs and climbers can quickly take over trellis divides, turning them into gloomy tangles of stems such as this one.

2. Trim back the climber to reveal the main stems and free them from the timber of the trellis. If you're working with Firethorn, wear thick gardening gloves.

3. Move the stems out of the way, mark a circle on the trellis with chalk and cut out with a saw.

4. Plait willow stems into a ring and tie into the moon gate with string. This gives the circle more definition, but if you don't have willow any woody plant with long whippy stems, such as dogwood or forsythia, will do.

5. Tie the stems back into the trellis, leaving a 10cm gap between them and the willow hoop. This space is important as it allows the stems to grow and makes pruning much easier later on.

Hazel Garden Screens

Garden screens are invaluable for disguising ugly sheds, walls and compost heaps but their uses don't end there. In design terms they divide gardens into different spaces, allowing various themes and changes of style to be developed independently, even where space is limited. They can be used, for example, to separate a children's play area and a flower garden. Screens made from hazel poles, like the one shown here, are infinitely adaptable and can be used to follow curves, cross paths and changes in height, depending on their purpose. They're strong, long-lasting and easy to move if you're the type of gardener who likes to chop and change things around and they're much cheaper than permanent structures such as fences and walls. Ideal in cottage, woodland and wild gardens, a hazel garden screen will add bags of rustic charm to any fenced suburban plot and they're quick and easy to construct.

You will need...

2m hazel poles, 10 for every metre of screen
Metal staking bar
Club hammer
Wire*
Pliers
Loppers/pruning saw

* Copper wire looks more ornamental

1. Make a line of holes by hammering the metal staking bar 20cm into the ground and wriggle it around to open up the sides of each hole. Make the holes roughly 10cm apart.

2. Then push a hazel rod down into each hole to make a line of uprights and firm back around with your foot to make sure they're solid.

3. Tie a hazel rod horizontally 1.5m up from the ground with string. Then bind each upright to it with wire.

4. To make an arch, bring the hazel screen up to each side of a path, bend a hazel pole into an arch and attach to the end uprights with copper wire.

5. Use loppers or a pruning saw to trim the tops of each pole level. Either cut them to the same level or at varying heights for a serpentine top.

Salad Leaf Boxes

This simple project will provide you with a supply of fresh baby salad leaves through the summer and into the autumn with minimal effort. Bags of salad leaves sold by supermarkets fetch premium prices, but you can avoid the cost by growing your own in boxes just outside the kitchen door. Grown in multipurpose compost away from the soil, the cut leaves don't pick up particles of soil and can be rinsed clean in seconds. If the boxes are set on a patio or deck they're less prone to slug attack and, come the autumn, can be moved into a porch or greenhouse to keep producing way beyond the first heavy frosts. Crops of leaves, such as loose-leaf lettuce, rocket and spinach, are ideal as they produce a succession of harvests re-growing from the cut stems. You don't need much space, just an open sunny position and the nearer the kitchen door, the better.

You will need...

Old wooden wine boxes or similar
Slow-release fertiliser capsules
Multi-purpose compost
Labels and seeds
Scissors for harvesting

1. Put the boxes in an open sunny position. Choose different spots depending on the time of year. In spring and autumn put them near a sunny wall to take advantage of the shelter and warmth it gives off.

2. Fill each box with multi-purpose compost to 3cm from the top and add two slow-release fertiliser capsules to each. The fertiliser is released as the plants need it and encourages lots of tender leafy growth.

3. Use a watering can with a rose on its spout to wet the compost and then sow the salad seeds evenly across the surface, one variety per box, with roughly 3cm gaps between them. Label each box to remind you what they are later.

4. Sprinkle a 1mm layer of dry compost on top and leave to grow, watering well in dry weather and keeping an eye out for slugs. Cut the leaves level with the top of the box when harvesting, leaving the base of the plants to re-grow.

Halloween Lanterns

Tip... Pumpkin lanterns last longer if they are left to dry out overnight before a candle is lit inside them. Also, the shorter the candle the slower the lid will be to shrivel and become floppy.

There is something about making pumpkin lanterns that appeals to adults and children alike. It's a creative salute to the changing seasons, with the pumpkin crop sown in high summer decorating the dark nights of autumn.

Making Halloween lanterns is a tradition that originates in Ireland, where turnips were carved with ghoulish faces to ward off evil spirits. When Irish emigrants settled in America, they took the tradition with them but found the ubiquitous pumpkin much easier to work and exported the idea back to the UK.

Nowadays, both garden centres and supermarkets sell good-sized pumpkins for the purpose, or you can sow seed directly into a sunny spot in May for a late summer harvest. The best variety to sow is the large orange and aptly named 'Halloween', but any good-sized squash or pumpkin will do.

To cut complicated scenes of witches flying across moonlit skies or grinning Cheshire Cats, you can make your own cutting tool from a coping saw blade (see step 1). They are simple to make and safer than a knife.

You will need...

Coping saw blade
Pliers
Wooden dowel
Drill and pilot bit

All-surface marker pen
Spoon
Pumpkins and candles

1. Drill a hole 2cm deep in the end of a length of dowel. Cut a coping saw blade in half with pliers and push into the hole.

2. Draw out a design on paper and copy it onto the skin of the pumpkin with a marker pen. Then, for the lid, draw a circle around the stalk wide enough for a hand to pass through.

3. Cut around the lid with the saw keeping the blade at roughly 45 degrees. This is important to stop the cut lid falling in on top of the candles.

4. Remove the lid and scoop out the insides of the pumpkin with a spoon. Save the seeds to grow your own pumpkins next year by storing them in a paper envelope in a dry dark place.

5. Cut out the design with the saw, angling the blade to remove as much flesh as possible, particularly behind detailed lines such as cats' whiskers and broomsticks. Put a candle in the base and wait until nightfall to light.

Devon Bank

The tall, thick hedges that line the sides of country lanes in the West Country are known locally as Devon Banks, as beneath the tangled stems there's a stone wall with a soil-filled centre. The soil gives the wall extra weight, increasing its stability, and allows grasses and hedging plants, such as hawthorn and Dog Roses, to root and bind the stones together.

In a garden, a Devon Bank makes a superb divide and provides an opportunity to naturalise hedgerow wildflowers like primroses, daffodils, foxgloves and violas. A turf top makes it evergreen and can be cut with shears for a neat 'cattle-grazed' look or simply left to grow shaggy and long.

Alternatively, a Devon Bank makes an ideal home for rock plants such as Sweet William, arabis and aubrieta which will spill down its face and look far more natural than on a conventional rockery.

And best of all, you don't need a quarry-load of stone, as even a short serpentine wall situated in a border recreates that country lane charm.

You will need...

Rockery/old walling stone
Top soil
Leaky hosepipe
Turf
Foxgloves, primroses, violas and
 spring bulbs or alpine plants

1. Mark out the line of the wall and dig out a trench 10cm deep and 60cm wide. The width may need to be greater if the stones are large. Lay out all the stones on the ground near to where you are working so you can see their size and shape for fast selection as you build.

2. Make two rows of the largest stones along the front and back of the wall, positioning them so their tops slope towards the centre of the wall. Then pack soil between them.

3. Place the second row of stones over the joints of the bottom course and a few centimetres back from the top edge of the first. If necessary, wedge small stones underneath any that rock and pack with soil.

4. Every 2m place a long stone across the wall to 'tie' the two faces together.

5. Keep adding stones and back filling with soil. Ensure that each course sits back from the edge of the one below, so that the wall gets narrower as it gets taller.

6. Once the wall is at the desired height – no more than 90cm for safety – put a leaky hosepipe down the centre to make watering easier and cover with soil.

7. Lay lengths of turf on the top of the wall and plant a few tufts into the gaps on the sides. Plant up with violas, foxgloves and primroses.

Leaf Curtains

Tip... Flat and leathery leaves are the best for mobiles; they can be found on Vines, Maples and tulip trees (Liriodendron tulipifera), the latter seen here framed in a loop of dogwood.

Autumn is one of the seasons that can pass you by all too quickly, especially if you're in an office all day. The nights draw in rapidly and wind and rain often whisk away its beauty. But if you have little time to go out and enjoy the turning trees then bring them close up with a curtain of leaves near your window. It's an ideal way to enjoy the amazingly rich spectrum of colours, close to hand, and a good excuse for collecting leaves in the park especially if you have kids. The leaves will brighten dull windows and keep you in touch with this most magical of seasons.

Make designs that fit your window from leaves collected from trees near your home. Oiling the leaves with petroleum jelly prevents drying out and helps to keep their colours bright.

You will need...

Leaves
Petroleum hand cream or jelly
Fishing line/nylon thread
Twigs/thin branches

Autumn colour...

As the temperature drops in autumn, trees and shrubs stop producing chlorophyll – the green pigment that enables them to turn sunlight into energy. As the chlorophyll becomes diluted other pigments such as yellow and orange carotenoids and red anthocyanins are revealed and the trees take on their autumn tints.

1. Collect leaves as soon as possible after they have fallen and dry off the surface with tissue paper. Then place between the pages of a telephone directory. Put this on the floor and stack three or four heavy books on top.

2. Every two days, move the leaves to a different, dry part of the directory and re-stack the books on top. They should be ready after about a week when they are dry but still slightly soft and rubbery. Remove and rub a thin coating of petroleum jelly over both sides of the leaf.

3. Cut the nylon thread into lengths 30–60cm long and tie one end to each of the leaf stalks.

4. Tie the other end to a twig to make a mobile and fix in front of a sheltered window with tacks or drawing pins. To help keep the colour in the leaves, re-apply petroleum jelly every two to three weeks.

Plant Theatre

Plant theatres are a traditional way of displaying the delicate beauty of pot-grown primroses and auriculas, bringing their dainty painted petals up to eye level where they can be enjoyed, whilst keeping them protected from spring winds and rain. They make great displays for all sorts of plants and are ideal in gardens where patio or window-sill space is limited or for keeping precious pot plants out of reach of pets and children.

If you like to ring the changes, you can have colour in the theatre year-round. In winter fill the shelves with Winter Aconites and snowdrops, followed by crocuses and primulas in the spring. Geraniums can add summer colour and cyclamen takes centre stage in autumn.

You will need...

5.5m of planed 1.5cm x 12cm timber
50cm of 2cm x 1.5cm batten
Pot of wood stain
20 2cm wood screws
Drill and pilot bit
Screwdriver
Jigsaw with a fine blade
Cross-cutting saw

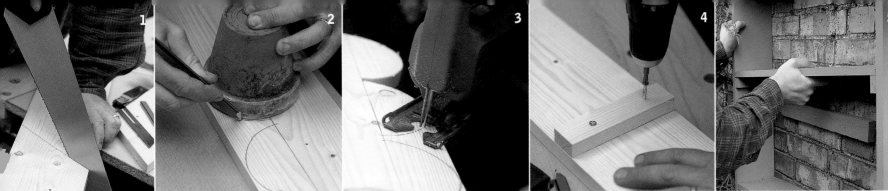

1. Mark and cut the timber following the cutting plan shown below. To get the slope of the roof the same on both sides, cut the top of one side at a 45 degree angle, then use it as a pattern for the other side.

2. Use a plant pot as a stencil to mark out the scalloped front edge of the roof leaving 1cm gaps between each semicircle to make manoeuvring the jigsaw easier.

3. Cut the scalloped front edge of the roof with a jigsaw fitted with a fine blade. The trick to using the jigsaw accurately is to push the saw slowly, stopping and changing your standing position regularly so you stay comfortable and can see the line you are cutting.

4. Cut 4 12cm lengths of batten and screw one at the base and one halfway up each side. Then screw the shelves down onto these and the roof to the tops of the uprights. It's easier and neater if you pilot a hole with a thin drill bit before you screw.

5. Paint the plant theatre and fix to the wall either with metal brackets or by screwing a length of batten to the wall, sitting the top shelf on it and screwing through the shelf into the baton.

Log Torches

Everyone loves the warm orange glow given off by the flickering flames of a bonfire, but not every garden is big enough or suitable because of overhanging trees and branches. However, it is possible to recreate the same warmth and ambience with timber torches made from cut logs.

They work much the same as a chimney, with a draft fanning a fire that burns in the centre of the log, carrying its flame up and over its top where it dances like a torch. Because there's more of a draft above the log, air is always drawn in through the bottom and flames out from the top. The wood burns from the inside out and produces a torch for 2–4 hours depending on the type and size of the wood. Once the sides have burned away the through-draft is lost causing the log to cool and the flame to disappear leaving just glowing embers.

The best logs come from conifer trees, as the resin in the wood helps them to burn. However, any timber can be used as long as it's completely dry, so keep in a cupboard indoors for a few weeks to dry it out before burning or buy dried logs from tree surgeons.

You will need...

30cm tall x 20cm wide dry log
Drill and auger bit or a 20cm wood bit
Tea candle

Safety precaution...

Once alight the log must be kept on the ground away from any other flammable materials. Whenever you have a fire of any kind in the garden, always keep a bucket of water or a hosepipe on standby to put out the fire if necessary. Never leave a fire unattended.

1. Stand the log up on its end and drill a cluster of holes two thirds of the way down through its centre. Move the bit around to join the holes up to make a single hole 4cm in diameter.

2. Lay the log on its side and drill another 4cm hole that meets up with the base of the first.

3. Cut the top centimetre off a candle using a sharp knife: this stops the wax crumbling and keeps the wick intact.

4. Put the log back up on its end, hole side up, in a sheltered spot out of the wind. Light the candle and push it to the back of the hole. Once the wood is alight, move onto a lawn or path where the torch can burn without risk of the fire spreading.

The loss of leaves means that th

garden is reduced to basic shapes and forms. What colour there is, from winter bulbs or bark, seems all the brighter in the low winter light.

Branches and rose stems are exposed and ready for pruning both for ornament now and for more flowers and fruit later.

The garden is at its least cluttered, making it easier to set out and see new designs and, as long as the ground is not frozen, move small trees, shrubs and flowers and plant new ones.

Winter is a wonderful time to tackle large projects in anticipation of the growing season and the physical work will keep you warm.

But if it's too cold to venture out for long there's plenty you can do to bring the garden indoors and to brighten up the views from your window.

Winter

Cottage Garden Path

A brick path is a beautiful garden feature, conjuring up images of rambling cottage gardens. Even if new bricks are used, the path looks like it's been there for ages, particularly when cottage garden plants spill onto its edges.

The path shown here can be built straight into soil and no brick-laying skills are needed. Any old bricks can be used, although the easiest to work with don't have 'frogs' (recesses on their undersides) and so sit flatter on the ground. The pattern shown here is known as a 'stretcher bond', so called because all the bricks run in the same direction. It's much easier to lay than other designs, for example 'herringbone', which requires lots of brick cutting, and 'basket-weave', which won't follow curved designs.

You will need...

Bricks (approximately 45 per
 square metre of path)
Sharp sand (1 25kg bag per
 1.5m of path)
A piece of timber no wider than
 the path to screed the sand level

Cutting bricks to length...

Where the ends of the path butt up to another solid surface, such as a patio, bricks can be cut to fit the gap. Do this is with a brick bolster, a chisel-like tool with a 5–10cm wide blade filed to a blunt point. Use the bolster to mark a line around the brick where you want the cut to follow. Then put a cushion of sand about 2cm thick onto soil and sit the brick side-up on the sand. Rest the edge of the blade on the line you want cut. Make a sharp hit to the bolster with a hammer and if it doesn't break flip the brick over onto its other edge and do the same again. Repeat until the brick is cut. Wear goggles and gloves for protection.

1. With a hosepipe or length of rope, mark out the sides of the path. To make laying the bricks easier later on, make the path roughly 10cm wider than you need it. Then dig out its base to roughly the depth of a brick.

2. Firm the bottom with your feet and rake the soil flat, picking out any stones and cutting off any protruding roots.

3. Shovel sharp sand into the base and screed flat with a straight-edged piece of timber until it's between 1–2cm deep. Sharp sand makes the best path base as, unlike other types of sand, it has angular grains that lock together creating a firm bed.

4. Place the bricks in position on the sand along the length of the path.

5. To get them perfectly level with each other, put a piece of wood on their tops and hammer down on the wood, working section by section along the path.

6. Back-fill soil to the path edge packing it firmly against the bricks with a stick or hammer handle.

7. Brush sharp sand over the path until the joints are full. This locks them firmly together and prevents any movement.

Ornamental Potager

A potager is an ornamental vegetable garden laid out in a symmetrical pattern with paths intersecting soil-filled beds. Flowers grow in among vegetables to attract bees that pollinate the crops and pest predators such as hoverflies and ladybirds, which hunt down aphids and other plant-eating insects. The symmetry of the garden keeps it looking good both in winter, when few crops occupy the soil, and summer, when strawberries and nasturtiums spill onto the paths and the beds are full of vegetables. The sides of each bed in my potager have been shuttered with timber giving the whole design a neat, crisp look. It also allows the soil to be piled deeper in the beds improving the growing conditions.

You will need*...

Tannalised timber planks
 1.5cm thick x 15cm wide
50mm x 30mm tannalised timber
 batten for pegs
1 40cm peg for every 120cm
 of shuttering
25mm galvanised flat-head nails
Wood saw
Spade
Compost to dig into beds
Gravel for the paths (1 40kg bag
 covers just over 1sq metre)

* The total length of shuttering is dictated by your plan

Vegetable growing

Vegetables are very easy to grow from seed even for inexperienced gardeners. If plants are watered and protected from slugs it's not hard to get good crops from any reasonably fertile soil. And once you've tasted sweetcorn or runner beans harvested from your garden there will be no going back: you'll want to grow more. To get the best vegetables invest in a good growing book, which will give you advice on soil pH, crop rotation and maximising your harvest for many years to come.

1. Mark out your plan with bamboo canes and string lines making sure the paths and beds are the right size. Dig out the paths to a depth of 10cm, piling the soil in the middle of the beds, and hammer wooden pegs into the ground along their edge using the string lines to keep them straight. The pegs form the supports for the edge of the raised beds.

2. Cut the timber shuttering to length and prop against the pegs, making sure that they're level.

3. Then nail into position, supporting the back of the peg with a spade.

4. Build up the design regularly, checking that the paths are straight and the beds square. If you're making a circle like the one in this design, put this in last.

5. To get the borders ready for sowing, dig compost into the soil – a barrowful for every 2m, and firm gently with the flats of your feet and then rake level. Flatten out the paths and cover with gravel.

Continued over >

Design tips

Choose a sunny site for your potager and measure its dimensions. Then make a plan of the site on paper and experiment with designs that will fit your plot. Make the beds 120cm wide so that all parts of them can be reached from the paths. This means that sowing, weeding and harvesting can be achieved without standing on the soil. As well as being convenient, this prevents the soil getting compacted underfoot keeping it soft, airy and easy for plants to root through. For easy access, make the paths wide enough for a wheelbarrow to sit comfortably between the beds. Bear in mind that beds with straight edges are straightforward to build, while curved and circular designs look fabulous but require extra woodworking skills to make.

Making wooden circles

Making straight planks bend isn't difficult if you follow these simple steps.

1. Mark cutting lines across the planks with a pencil. The closer the lines, the more the wood will bend once cut. For a 1.8m diameter circle, make them 10cm apart.

2. Cut along the lines, four-fifths of the way through the wood with a saw. To save time use a circular saw.
Take the ends of the plank and gently bend it with the cuts on the inside of the curve. The wood should make snapping noises as the sides of each cut come together. Once you have an even curve, cut to length and fix into position.

Copper Obelisk

Tip... The tops can be decorated with finials too: pebbles, terracotta pots, shiny deer-scarers and balls wound from copper wire.

Copper piping from plumbers' merchants can be used to make obelisks. When new and shiny, they stand out in borders like pieces of modern art. Then as the copper ages, it burnishes and takes on warm hues, eventually turning copper blue or verdigris. In all its shades, it complements the natural colours found in gardens, those of leaves, bark, stonework and timber year-round. Also, it won't rot or rust so it's perfect for the garden, lasting indefinitely. I use copper obelisks to brighten up shady borders where their shine is accentuated. Clematis can use them as an escape route from the shade at ground level to the brighter light above.

Copper pipe can be bought from builders' merchant and plumbing stores in a range of diameters. If you're making a small obelisk, for example 60–100cm tall, thinner diameter pipes will look more in scale.

You will need*...

3 2m lengths of 22mm copper pipe
10m of 8mm copper boiler tube
2m role of copper wire
Step ladder
Gloves and pliers

* For a 1.8m obelisk

1. Push the copper pipes into the ground making a triangle with equal sides about 45cm long. Tie the tops together with the copper wire. If you find that the wire slips, use sticky tape to bind the tops of the pipes and then use the wire to hide the tape.

2. The boiler tube, which is sold in flat coils, goes on next. Take the end at the centre of the coil and bend it over on its self to make a hook roughly 10cm long. Standing on step ladders put the 'hook' inside one of the pipes and let the outside of the coil drape down over the obelisk.

3. Starting at the top, wrap the copper around the uprights, working your way downwards. Because copper anneals or gets harder when it's bent, try to curve as much as you can into position in one smooth movement. Bending a little at a time makes it harder to get the lines of the spiral kink free.

4. Once you've gone all the way down to the ground, adjust the copper so that the gaps between the spirals are the same, or gradually increasing, and fix them in position by tying them to uprights with copper wire. Any excess boiler tube can be cut off with pliers.

5. The tops can be decorated with finials too: pebbles, pots, balls of copper wire and shiny deer-scarers.

Winter Twiggery

In winter, gaps in the border become all too apparent as herbaceous plants die down and bedding plants are killed by the frosts. Replace the losses by cutting a few stems from plants with prettily coloured bark from elsewhere in the garden to add instant colour that will last right through the winter.

A twiggery is especially appropriate if you prefer a minimal look rather than traditional winter flowers, such as pansies and polyanthus. It is particularly useful for brightening up shady or soil-less corners where plants don't thrive. What is more, creating an outdoor arrangement like this also acts as a propagator, as the stems often root. You'll know if they do as they grow away in spring; in this case, cut them back by two thirds, so that the proportion of root to shoot is balanced, tease from the pot and plant in the garden.

You will need...

Secateurs
Top soil
Terracotta pot
Plants with bright winter stems such as
 Kerria japonica, dogwood, jasmine, willow,
 bamboo (if the leaves are cut off) and acers

1. Prune a few stems from shrubs with brightly coloured winter bark. If you only take a couple from each plant you won't notice they've gone.

2. Position the pot where you want the twiggery and fill with soil. If you're using a tall pot, dig a hole a few inches deep and bury its base for extra stability.

3. Push the twigs into the soil until they touch the bottom of the pot; splay them out to catch the sun. Keep the soil moist to help anchor the pot and to encourage the twigs to root.

Training Roses

Finished look... The willow circles are tied to taut wire supports that hold them proud of the wall. When the sun shines, shadows play across the brickwork, doubling the ornamental effect.

From June right through until the first frosts of autumn, climbing roses provide a spectacular show of blooms. They make good cut flowers: some are sweetly scented and many produce attractive red hips that last on the plant into the depths of winter. If trained, the stems become ornamental features in their own right enhancing the plant's appearance year-round.

Scrappy 'birds nests' of briars can be transformed into living sculptures and, if done properly, the plant will flower more freely and be less susceptible to disfiguring fungal diseases such as black spot and mildew.

Climbing roses should always be tied into something solid. For this rose I fixed wires to a wall and made a framework of willow hoops to increase the ornamental effect and to make tying-in easier.

You will need...

Bundle of willow
Tar-impregnated twine
Garden twine
Secateurs
Step ladder
Gloves

Climbing rose care

Roses grown against a wall need extra care to help them establish. This is because the bricks in the wall absorb moisture from the soil and the wall itself casts a rain shadow. Therefore, plant at least 50cm away from the wall training the rose back towards it and mulch annually with a 10cm layer of well-rotted farmyard manure.

1. Take the rose down from its old supports, gently flopping it on to the ground and fix new wire supports in position if necessary. (*see* Training Wires for Climbers, page 34).

2. To make the rose more manageable, thin any old and spindly branches and cut back side shoots to two buds from the main stem. The rose will send up next year's flower spikes from these buds.

3. Make hoops by bending willow rods into circles and tying their ends together with string.

4. Wrap two or three more willow rods around the hoop to make it rigid and to hide the string.

5. Tie the hoops to the wires with tar-impreganted twine. For this helix design, I started with a small hoop in the centre and built up a spiral of ever-growing hoops around it.

6. Tie the rose to the hoops with soft twine, leaving 12cm gaps between the stems. Keep the stems as horizontal as you can: the flatter they are, the more flower buds they'll produce. Avoid pushing the stems behind the wires or hoops as this makes future pruning and tying-in difficult.

Fossil Sculpture

Having children doesn't mean your garden needs be turned over to an assortment of plastic toys. It is possible to both stimulate their imaginations and have a pretty plot if you use natural materials to create play areas.

This dinosaur 'fossil' is the perfect project for budding paleontologists and is simply made from sliced-up logs and branches. The wood can be cut to any size depending on the branches you have, but bear in mind that large pieces of timber will need to be cut by a chainsaw. Once the pieces are cut, the kids can enjoy positioning them into a fossil shape. Alternatively, you may want to make it yourself as an exciting surprise for them. Eventually, the wood, if left untreated, will rot down into the soil. But in the meantime it's a good solution for difficult-to-plant, dry areas around hedge bases and trees.

You will need...

Branches of varying thickness
Bow saw/chainsaw
Spade and trowel

Jurassic path...

Dinosaur designs can also be incorporated into paths and patios. The simplest way is to set the log slices into the soil and surround with bark chippings or gravel. For a permanent feature, incorporate rot-resistant hardwoods such as oak, slices of treated timber stakes or telegraph poles among cobbles or granite setts.

1. Cut the logs into slices 10cm thick. If you only have a few branches you can cut them thinner but they won't last as long.

2. Set the logs out on the ground in the pattern you want. It's a good idea to get the backbone and tail in place first, as these are the most eye-catching, and dictate where the legs and head go.

3. Once you're happy with the design, dig a hole for each log and set each into the soil with its top just above ground level.

4. Firm the logs into position by packing soil around them with a trowel or a short length of wood.

Willow Tree Seat

Gardening with natural materials is wonderful as they are easy to use and so pleasurable to work with. Structures made from them blend with their surroundings regardless of whether the garden is contemporary or old-fashioned. Contrasted with glass and metal in a modern garden, the beauty and individuality of the materials is enhanced, while natural materials such as hazel, willow, and shaggy turf complement a cottage garden perfectly.

I've made two different formats to try and both make superb focal points (see the Lover's Bench, page 122). The tree seat is based on the grassy hummocks used for courting in medieval gardens, which had brick, plank or willow edges and wild flowers and herbs mixed in with the grass.

You will need*...

2 bundles of willow
10 2.5m hazel rods
5m of turf
4 barrows of topsoil
5m of micro-irrigation hosepipe
Hosepipe end connector
Lump hammer
Secateurs
Loppers

* Makes a 1.5m wide tree seat

Tree care...

Never stack soil up against the trunk of a tree as it will block microscopic air holes in the bark essential for healthy growth and can even kill large trees. So, when building a tree seat, ensure that the inner wall is at least 45cm out from the trunk. This is not only good for the tree, but makes it easier to hammer the pegs into the soil.

1. Mark two circles in the soil around the base of a tree, the inner one 60cm out from the trunk and the outer circle 1m. Then cut the hazel rods into 40cm lengths and hammer them into the ground following the circles, leaving gaps of 20cm between them.

2. Once all of the pegs are in, take handfuls of willow (about 9 rods), and weave them in and out of the pegs taking care to pack the rods down tightly. Make up the inner circle first to practise, as mistakes here won't show when the seat is finished.

3. Make up the outer circle, packing the willow to reduce the number of gaps and for strength.

4. Then make up the outer circle as shown.

Continued over >

The use of low willow walls, filled with soil and topped with turf isn't restricted to tree seats. I've used them to make football-proof boundaries to lawns, as serpent-shaped seats in children's gardens and as economical walls for raised planting beds. The materials are so adaptable and easy to work with the opportunities are endless. You could use them to disguise ugly concrete walls to make a mini maze or as a seat around a raised pond. As long as the soil inside them is kept moist, the willow edges will stay supple and strong and whatever structure you make will last for years.

5. Fill the space between the circles with topsoil, firming it as you go.

6. To make watering the grass on the seat easier, lay a micro-irrigation pipe into the top few centimetres of soil. Block one end up and attach a universal hosepipe clip to the other.

7. Poke the end with the hose clip out through the inner wall of the seat on a side which won't be seen. When the grass needs a drink simply plug a hosepipe to the seat and turn on.

8. Because the soil will settle, over fill the seat by about 10cm. Lay the turf on top, tucking the edges down inside the seat. Keep well watered until the turf has established and clip from time to time with garden shears.

Lovers' Bench

Unlike an ordinary garden bench that directs your gaze out into the garden, a lovers' seat is crafted to allow two people to face each other and even lean forward to kiss... This lovers' seat is based on the smooth lines of classic metalwork designs and makes an instant piece of garden sculpture. Build where it will be chanced upon, such as beneath a bower of roses or in the shade of a tree, or position in the open where it will become an attractive focal point inviting you to sit. Either way, this woven love seat will make your garden a more romantic place.

Tip... To make watering easier, build a micro-irrigation system into the seat. For details see Willow Tree Seat, page 120 (step 7).

You will need...

Bundle of willow
12 2.5m hazel poles
3 barrows of topsoil
5m of turf
3m of micro-irrigation hose

1. Mark an 'S' shape on the soil and hammer 1m long hazel poles along it. Leave 10cm gaps between them and splay the rods so they lean out slightly from the centre of the seat.

2. Cut the poles to length leaving the backs of the two seats about 1m tall with sides that slope gently down towards the fronts.

3. Hammer in more hazel pegs to form the fronts of the seats. Keep these upright and just under knee height when hammered in firmly.

4. Build the sides next by weaving individual lengths of willow in and out of the hazel poles. Work your way around the seat adding extra willow to low areas when necessary until you've reached the tops of the poles at the fronts.

Continued over >

If you want flowery cushions on your love seat, plant daisies and buttercups into the turf, taking care when cutting the grass not to remove their flower heads. Alternatively, if your seat is in a sunny spot, use scented herbs such as camomile or thyme to cover the cushions. Although not as hard-wearing as grass, if planted densely with a 1cm layer of horticultural grit brushed between them, they will cope with a certain amount of sitting, releasing their herby aroma into the air. For perfume around the seat, plant scented roses, sweet rocket, mignonettes and heliotropes or train a honeysuckle to clamber up the backs.

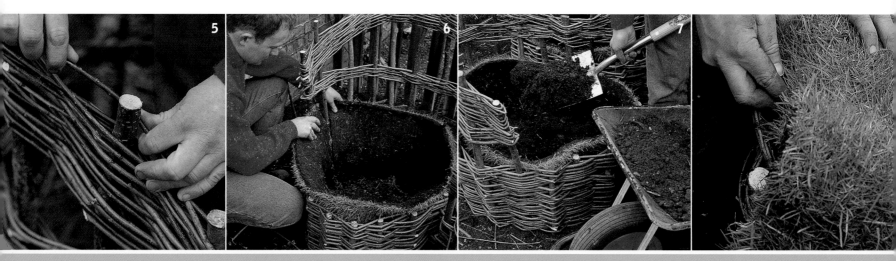

5. Weave two bands of willow along the backs to complete the frame. When you reach the ends bend the willow rods around the last hazel pole and weave back in the opposite direction.

6. Line the inside of the seat with turf. This will eventually grow away, giving the seat soft green sides and it prevents soil leaking out from between the willow.

7. Fill the inside of the seat with topsoil, firming it with your feet as you go.

8. Dome up the soil in the centre of the seats to give the appearance of cushions and turf over the top. Water the grass to help it establish and keep watered in dry weather.

Apple Tree Pots

Pruning and training...
Pruning and training will dramatically increase the harvest of apples and keep the tree compact. In the first year after planting, the idea is to create an evenly spaced framework of major branches. This might mean removing any that cross or tying them into a new position with string. Vertical branches can be tied down too as this will reduce their vigour and encourage them to produce extra flowers and fruit.

Once a framework of evenly spaced branches is established, prune the new summer growth to five or six leaves in late July: the new growth is recognisable because it's straight and has no fruit forming on it. In winter, prune these side shoots again just above the second or third bud.

If you are a patio or balcony gardener, you needn't limit the range of plants you grow to summer bedding and winter pansies. A productive and interesting alternative is an apple tree grown in a pot. It adds height, is permanent and gives the garden a whole new dimension. An apple tree will mark the seasons with spring blossom that swells into apples through the summer until ready for picking in autumn. There are hundreds of varieties to choose from, each with a different flavour and harvest period. Some, like 'Discovery', are ready for picking in September while varieties like 'Sturmer Pippin' ripen on the tree until late winter. If you have an apple tree in your garden, growing a variety that ripens at a different time in a pot will extend the harvest period.

Feed and water the tree through the growing season and, for extra colour, plant flowers and bulbs around its base.

You will need...

1m tree stake and tie
50cm half-barrel
80L of compost (preferably a 50/50 mix
 of multi-purpose and John Innes No3)
Apple tree
Crocks or stones for drainage

Choosing a variety

Every apple tree is sold on a range of rootstocks that determine how large the mature tree will grow. For growing in a pot choose a variety on a dwarfing or semi-dwarfing stock to encourage early fruiting and to prevent it taking over the patio. Apple trees aren't self-fertilising and if you live in an area where ther are no other apple trees nearby, you'll need to grow at least two trees to ensure pollination. Your local nursery will advise on suitable varieties.

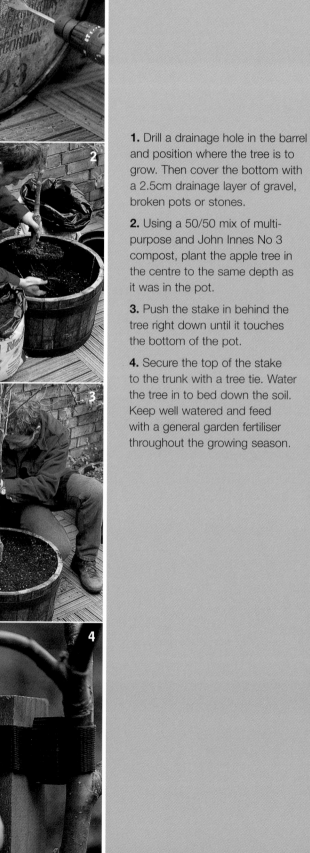

1. Drill a drainage hole in the barrel and position where the tree is to grow. Then cover the bottom with a 2.5cm drainage layer of gravel, broken pots or stones.

2. Using a 50/50 mix of multi-purpose and John Innes No 3 compost, plant the apple tree in the centre to the same depth as it was in the pot.

3. Push the stake in behind the tree right down until it touches the bottom of the pot.

4. Secure the top of the stake to the trunk with a tree tie. Water the tree in to bed down the soil. Keep well watered and feed with a general garden fertiliser throughout the growing season.

Fan-trained Cherry in a Pot

Cherry tree care...
During the growing season keep the compost moist and feed regularly with a general liquid fertiliser. New growth at the ends of the branches should be tied in to the canes every couple of months. If one branch outgrows all the rest, cutting off the end 10cm, just above a bud will increase the flow of sap to the other branches, speeding up their growth.

Alternatively, untie the branch from the wire supports and re-secure in a more horizontal position. Again this will slow its growth and redirect sap to the other branches. After a few weeks, when they have caught up, tie back in the original position.

Many gardens have narrow alleys leading out from the back door and it's a headache finding something that will thrive in this dark and often soil-less area. The solution I used was a trained 'Morello' cherry tree in a barrel. Its branches have a beautiful symmetry and, although flat to the wall, it still provides all the dynamic interest of a fully grown tree with fruit to boot.

In winter its branches resemble the ribs of a giant leaf and, as spring approaches, the buds fatten bursting into leaf then flowers and fruit. In summer, why not plant a skirt of bedding around its base and winter pansies in the autumn when the leaves on the tree turn butter-yellow.

Fan-trained 'Morello' cherry trees are available from garden centres and fruit nurseries and are sold on a variety of rootstocks. As its name suggests, a rootstock is the part of the plant that sits below the soil and governs how big the tree grows. The type to buy for this project is a dwarfing stock called 'Colt', which stays relatively compact without masses of pruning.

You will need...

Fan-trained 'Morello' cherry on 'Colt' stock
60cm half-barrel
John Innes No 3 and multi-purpose compost
10 2m bamboo canes
Garden twine

Pruning

Cherries form on one-year-old shoots produced the previous summer. Pruning involves cutting back fruited side-shoots and replacing them with new growth that will fruit next year. Prune after harvest when the weather is dry to avoid infection from the fungal disease silver leaf that spreads in wet weather.

1. Paint the walls with white masonry paint to increase the light levels and give the cherry tree a bright backdrop.

2. Drill a hole in the barrel and place it against the wall, covering its base with a drainage layer of stones or rocks. Plant the cherry at the back of the barrel so that the branches fan out against the wall.

3. Fix training wires to the wall with the lowest wire level with the lowest branch of the tree when it is bent down horizontally.

4. Tie bamboo canes to the wires in a fan shape corresponding to the main branch framework. Then tie the branches to the bamboo canes using soft garden twine. Water the tree to settle the compost around the roots.

Christmas Daffodils

The beauty of pot-grown bulbs like hyacinths and daffodils is that they can be brought in from the garden just as they are coming into flower and put back outside once the blooms are over. Their versatility makes them ideal for brightening up the house during winter and they have the added bonus of sweetly scented flowers. Give indoor pots a modern fresh look with this simple economical project.

You will need...

Pots of flowering bulbs such as
 'Tête-à-Tête', 'Paper White' and
 'Tazetta' daffodils or hyacinths.
Roll of tin foil
Sheet of thin card
Sticky tape
Moss
Ivy
1m of wire

Grow your own

Pot grown daffodils and hyacinths are available from garden centres from autumn through till late spring, but you can grow your own by planting autumn-bought bulbs in 3L pots of multi-purpose compost. For hyacinths, plant three bulbs per pot with their noses just proud of the compost surface. For daffodils, cover the bottom of the pot with 2–3cm of compost and put a ring of five bulbs around the edge. Cover these bulbs with compost and put another ring of five bulbs over this, then fill to the top with compost. By planting two layers of bulbs you'll get two flushes of flower.

To bring them into flower early, stand the pots in a cold greenhouse or porch and keep the compost moist.

1. Wrap the outside of the pot with tin foil covering the drainage holes in the base and tucking the excess around the rim. The foil stops water leaking from the pot and staining the table or window sill it sits on.

2. Bend a hoop in the middle of the wire roughly the size of the rim of the pot, with the two ends bent at right angles from it. Push the ends down the inside of the pot making sure all the foliage and flower spikes are held in the hoop.

3. Disguise the wire by wrapping ivy around it. It doesn't matter if the ends of the ivy don't reach the compost as the ivy will stay green for weeks even without water.

4. Cut a length of card long enough to wrap around the pot and a few centimetres wider than the pot is tall. Lay this on a sheet of foil and fold the foil back over the card to cover it completely.

5. Wrap the foil-covered card around the pot and fix with sticky tape and cover the surface of the compost with moss.

Ice Mobiles

It's on winter days when the ground is covered in frost and the air is crisp that ice mobiles can be hung outdoors to decorate trees. As quick to make as ice cubes, an ice mobile is made decorative with the addition of berries, leaves or seeds harvested from the garden, so even young children can get involved. Just like a snowman, it will last while the cold weather holds and melt when it gets warmer, releasing berries and seeds for birds to feast on.

An ice mobile can be made the same day or stored in the freezer in anticipation of a cold snap, then hung in the garden where they can be seen from the house.

NB Always tell children not to eat berries picked from the garden.

You will need...

Water-tight tin foil containers (large tea candle cases are used here)
Berries, seeds and/or flowers
Wire or string

Birds and berries...

How quickly birds strip berries from garden plants changes from year to year with the weather and how much food is available elsewhere. As a general rule though, birds tend to eat the red berries first leaving the less palatable yellows, oranges and whites on the plants till last. Some red berries last better than others including the Firethorn Pyracantha 'Mohave', Cotoneaster lacteus and the hips of roses. For yellows you can't beat the holly Ilex 'Bacciflava or Pyracantha 'Soleil d'Or'.

1. Pick berries/seeds/flowers from the garden and put into aluminium containers half filling them up.

2. Bend wire into hoops kinking it so that the hoop sits flat onto the berries. Alternatively use hoops of string.

3. Wrap the end of the wire around the container so that less space is taken up in the freezer, fill with water and put in the freezer.

4. Wait for a cold day and hang outside from the branches of a tree.

Outdoor Candelabra

Fitting a fallen branch with glass tube hurricanes creates a natural-looking outdoor light.

Occasionally, fallen branches or tree prunings have such exquisite shapes or bark that they look like pieces of sculpture and, as such, have great potential in the garden. If you want something both artistic and practical, a wooden branch can be made into a rustic candleholder for permanent outdoor lighting, illuminating alfresco dinners and summer evening parties.

Although the glass cylinders surrounding the candles need to be specially ordered from a glass blower, it is no more expensive than the ubiquitous torch candles from garden centres. And these are totally original. Glass blowers or local glaziers can usually be found in the telephone directory. Tip... If the candle smoke is black and sooty, there is a lack of oxygen reaching the flame. Remedy this by drilling an air hole from the circle that the glass cylinder sits in through to the bottom of the log.

You will need...

Glass cylinders 4cm
 (internal diameter) x 25cm
Wooden log
Drill and drill bits
Hole-cutting bit
Chisel
Candles

1. Mark on the log where you want the candles to sit. Choose a smooth, level position as this makes drilling out easier.

2. Using a hole-cutting bit, drill out a hole that's slightly larger than the diameter of the cylinders. Then drill out a hole that's slightly smaller.

3. Use a chisel or sharp screwdriver to gouge out the circle of wood between the cuts. Aim to make this about 3cm deep.

4. Make holders for the candles by drilling down the centres of the circles with a 22mm bit to a depth of roughly 2cm.

5. Drill a hole right through to the base of the log. This allows the wax to escape if the candles burn right down. Always make sure these holes are clear before replacing burnt-down candles with new ones

6. Insert the candles in the centre hole, light and push the cylinders over them to protect the flame.

Glossary

Aquatic compost: a heavy, soil-based compost specially formulated for pond plants that doesn't float and contains only a small amount of fertiliser. Low nutrient levels in pond compost are essential as algae, which is always present in pond water, feeds and multiplies on any excess, turning the water pea-green. Subsoil, which also contains few nutrients, can be used as an alternative.

Auger bit: a drill fitting with a long shank for boring deep holes into wood.

Ballast: a naturally occurring mixture of sand and gravel that has been washed to remove impurities. Compacted ballast is used on its own as a sub-base for paving, or mixed with cement to make concrete.

Batten: a narrow length of wood.

Bitumastic paint: a water-proof paint used to seal surfaces susceptible to damage from moisture.

Bolt tensioners: metal bolts with a thread, washer and nut at one end and an eye at the other, used to pull training and fence wires taut. The wire is tied to the eye and the threaded bolt goes through a fence post or vine eye. The nut is threaded onto the bolt and as it is turned the bolt moves through it pulling the wire with it.

Bow saw: a saw used for cutting through large logs with a sprung 'C' shaped handle that holds a blade between its ends.

Cement: is made from ground limestone or chalk and clay and generally called Portland Cement. When mixed with soft sand (sand with round grains) and water it makes mortar and, when mixed with gravel and sharp sand (sand with angular grains), it makes concrete.

Chisel (wood): a tool with a square shank and sharp, bevelled end for shaping and hollowing out wood.

Club hammer: a hammer with a large, heavy rectilinear head, useful for driving bolsters when cutting bricks, clay pipes and flags, and demolition.

Concrete: a hard surface made from a mixture of cement, sand and gravel.

Coppicing: the ancient practice of felling trees and leaving the stump to regrow for future harvests. Coppicing is a technique used in the production of oak and ash poles, hazel rods and willow 'withies' used in basket weaving.

Cordons: a plant trained through regular pruning to have one main stem. This technique if often used on soft fruit trees but is also suitable for tomatoes.

Cross-cutting saw: also called a panel saw and used for cutting timber.

Dead-head: removing flowers as they fade to encourage the plant to produce more.

Disease-resistant: a plant that either naturally staves off diseases or has been bred to do so.

Dowel: a thin wooden rod

Drift: an undesirable airborne mist produced when spraying paints or chemicals, that causes pollution.

Feather board: timber planks used for fencing which taper across their width from 16mm down to 3mm allowing them to over-lap to create a solid boundary.

Fence spikes: metal fence spikes are a quick and easy alternative to concreting fence posts into the ground. Each has a long spike which anchors it in the soil and a square socket that the base of the fence post sits in.

Fibre board: made from compressed wood fibre pressed into sheets of various densities. Often used as insulation or as a packing material.

Floristry beads: rounded beads of coloured glass used as ornaments in vases and bowls and to anchor the stems of cut flowers.

Gaffer tape: strong, plastic, self-adhesive tape.

Galvanised wire: wire coated in zinc to prevent it from rusting.

Grouting blade: a tool available from DIY stores and tile suppliers, with a thin rubber blade for working cement into the gaps between tiles.

Hacksaw: a saw with a hardened blade and fine teeth, designed to cut metal.

Hand sprayer: a trigger-operated spray gun available from garden centres, used for misting houseplants and applying pesticides.

Heartwood: the dense inner core of a tree with the hardest wood.

Herbaceous: a term used to describe plants that have stems that die back each winter and roots that survive beneath the soil, sending up new shoots when the weather warms in spring.

Horticultural grit: washed angular grit that is added to compost to improve its drainage, or spread over the surface of compost in pots for ornament. Available from DIY stores and garden centres.

Jigsaw: a power-saw that can be used to cut timber boards and, if the appropriate blades are fitted, plastic and sheet metal. Because jigsaws are very manoeuvrable they are ideal for cutting curves and complicated shapes.

John Innes No3: a recipe for potting compost devised at the John Innes Horticultural Institution in Norwich in the UK containing sterilised top soil, peat, horticultural grit, lime and fertilizer.

Leader: the strongest and usually the uppermost branch of a plant

Leaky hose: perforated hosepipe that gently leaks water to irrigate plants.

Loppers: long handled secateurs with wide jaws for cutting branches from trees and shrubs.

Mallet (wooden): a hammer-like tool made of wood, for driving a chisel when cutting or hollowing out timber, or for hammering lengths of wood together without causing excessive damage to their surface.

Marginal plant: a water plant that naturally grows in the shallows at the edge of a pond or water course.

Marine ply: is made from thin veneers of timber stuck together under high pressure with waterproof glue. Available from timber merchants and DIY stores in sheets 244cm tall and 122cm wide ranging in thickness from 4 to 18mm. Half and quarter sheets are also available.

Masonry bit: a drill bit designed for making holes in bricks, concrete and stone.

Metal file: a finely milled file for removing sharp edges from cut metal.

Micro-irrigation pipe: hosepipe with tiny pores allowing water to seep from it at a controlled rate, ideal for irrigating borders and planters.

Mulch: a layer of compost, bark, gravel or any bulky material, over the surface of the soil. Mulches are beneficial as they can add nutrients, improve the organic content of the soil, keep down weeds, prevent moisture evaporating form the ground and they create a neat finish.

Multi-purpose compost: a potting compost recipe, based on either peat or bark with added lime and fertiliser.

Oxygenating plant: a pond plant that lives below the surface of the water and releases oxygen into it, essential for the life of the pond.

Pan: a planter that is shallow and wide, often used for growing plants that appreciate good drainage, like alpines and succulents.

Pilot Bit/Hole: a small guide hole drilled with a pilot bit, to make fixing screws easier.

Pollinate: to dust with pollen and fertilize in order to encourage the plant to produce seeds or fruit.

Pond liner: a plastic, PVC or butyl waterproof membrane.

Pond liner underlay: a soft sheet of material that stops stones or roots piercing the pond liner.

Pruning saw: a saw with a long thin blade for removing branches from trees and shrubs. Particularly useful where work space is limited.

Rootstock: used to provide the root part of a plant, when two plants are grafted together. Many ornamental trees, most fruit trees and roses are grafted onto a rootstock to control their growth rate.

Rubber mallet: a mallet with a soft face that won't mark the material being worked. Used to tap paving slabs into position, for bending metal and knocking wooden joints together.

Scoring blade: a Stanley/craft knife blade with a strong curved point that won't snap when scoring a line.

Screed: to smooth the surface of mortar or concrete with a straight-edged piece of wood.

Sharp sand: sand with angular grains ideal for concrete mixes as their sharp sides lock together making for a strong bond.

Shuttering: a retaining edge to hold in place loose aggregates, such as gravel or soil. Can be temporary or permanent.

Silicone glue: a versatile adhesive that dries to make a waterproof seal. Useful for gluing materials with smooth surfaces together, such as glass or metal.

Slow-release fertiliser: a plant food designed to release nutrients slowly over a number of months. Some are coated in a membrane that controls the amount of food released while others gradually degrade releasing nutrients into the soil. Sold from garden centres as granules and pellets.

Spars: the wooden uprights and cross members of trellis.

Spirit level: a tool for checking that surfaces are perfectly flat or upright.

Stanley knife: a knife with a changeable blade used for cutting, scoring and marking. Sometimes called a craft knife.

Subsoil: the inert soil that starts from 3cm to 30cm below the ground level, depending on the soil type. Distinct from topsoil which is usually darker in colour. Plants, (except pond plants and some wild flowers) don't like growing in it because it contains few plant nutrients.

Succulents: plants from any plant family that have swollen fleshy leaves to enable them to cope with drought.

Tannalised: timber that has been pressure-treated with preservative to stop it rotting when used outdoors.

Tin snips: a tool with large scissor blades for cutting sheet metals.

Topsoil: the top 10–30cm of soil containing plant nutrients, worms, fungi and bacteria essential for healthy plant growth. Topsoil is usually darker in colour than the subsoil that lies beneath it. When digging a hole for planting or making excavations, keep separate from the subsoil and return to the surface when work is finished.

Truss: a cluster of fruits or flowers.

Vine eyes: long screw with eyes at their ends for attaching training wires.

Wall plugs: plastic or wooden fittings that are pushed into drilled holes before screws driven into them. As the screw goes in, the plug expands to grip the sides of the hole.

Weed-suppressing membrane: a cloth that is laid on the soil surface to block out light and kill weeds. Unlike plastic sheeting, weed suppressing membranes don't restrict air movement or stop moisture passing through them, so can be planted through with ornamentals.

Index

Acknowledgements I'd like to thank: my wife Lisa, for all of her help, support, inspiration and gardening knowledge and her tolerance of the mud-stained carpets and the untidiness in our garden during the photography; Howard Rice for his organisational abilities, gardening knowledge, wood-working and craft skills, his fabulous photography and his tolerance of mud-stained carpets and the untidiness in his garden during the photography; my neighbours Annie, Gavin and their son Mark (pictured page 51) and Sally, not for mud-stained carpets but for tolerating the untidiness in their gardens during the photography and making Homerton Street such a lovely place to live. Thanks to Rosie and Simon for letting me build the Devon bank in their garden. And for running their building advice helplines, my dad and Chris.

Last but not least, thanks to all at Cassell for pulling it together so well.